Aquarius

21 January – 19 February

First published in Great Britain 2009
by Harlequin Mills & Boon Limited,
Eton House, 18-24 Paradise Road, Richmond, Surrey TW9 1SR

ISBN: 978 0 263 87074 9

Typeset at Midland Typesetters Australia

Harlequin Mills & Boon policy is to use papers that are natural, renewable and recyclable products and made from wood grown in sustainable forests. The logging and manufacturing processes conform to the legal environmental regulations of the country of origin.

Printed and bound in Spain
by Litografia Rosés S.A., Barcelona

About
Dadhichi

Dadhichi is one of Australia's foremost astrologers. He has the ability to draw from complex astrological theory to provide clear, easily understandable advice and insights for people who want to know what their future might hold.

In the 26 years that Dadhichi has been practising astrology, face reading and other esoteric studies, he has conducted over 9,500 consultations. His clients include celebrities, political and diplomatic figures, and media and corporate identities from all over the world.

Dadhichi's unique blend of astrology and face reading helps people fulfil their true potential. His extensive experience practising western astrology is complemented by his research into the theory and practice of eastern systems of astrology.

Dadhichi features in numerous newspapers and magazines and he also appears regularly on many of Australia's leading television and radio networks, where many of his political and worldwide forecasts have proved uncannily accurate.

His website www.astrology.com.au is now one of the top ten online Australian lifestyle sites and, in conjunction with www.facereader.com, www.soulconnector.com and www.psychjuice.com, they attract over half a million visitors monthly. The websites offer a wide variety of features, helpful information and personal services.

Dedicated to The Light of Intuition

Sri V. Krishnaswamy—mentor and friend

With thanks to Julie, Joram, Isaac and Janelle

Welcome from Dadhichi

Dear Friend,

Welcome! It's great to have you here, reading your horoscope, trying to learn more about yourself and what's in store for you in 2010.

I visited Mexico a while ago and stumbled upon the Mayan prophecies for 2012, which, they say, is the year when the longstanding calendar we use in the western world supposedly stops! If taken literally, some people could indeed believe that 'the end of the world is near'. However, I see it differently.

Yes, it might seem as though the world is getting harder and harder to deal with, especially when fear enters our lives. But, I believe that 'the end' indicated by these Mayan prophecies has more to do with the end that will create new beginnings for our societies, more to do with making changes to our material view of life and some necessary adjustments for the human race to progress and prosper in future. So let's get one thing straight: you and I will both be around after 2012, reading our 2013 horoscopes!

My prediction and advice centres around keeping a cool mind and not reacting to the fear that could overtake us. Of course, this isn't easy, especially when media messages might increase our anxiety about such things as the impacts of global warming or the scarcity of fossil fuels.

I want you to understand that it is certainly important to be aware and play your part in making the world a better place; however, the best and surest way to support global goals is to help yourself first. Let me explain. If everyone focused just a little more on improving *themselves* rather than just pointing their finger to criticise others, it would result in a dramatic change and improvement; not just globally, but societally. And, of course, you mustn't forget what a positive impact this would have on your personal relationships as well.

Astrology focuses on self-awareness; your own insights into your personality, thinking processes and relationships. This is why this small book you have in your hand doesn't only concentrate on what is going to happen, but more importantly how you can *make* things happen positively through being your best.

I have always said that there are two types of people: puppets and actors. The first simply react to each outside stimulus and are therefore slaves of their environment, and even of their own minds and emotions. They are puppets in the hands of karma. The other group I call actors. Although they can't control what happens to them all the time, either, they are better able to adapt and gain something purposeful in their lives. They are in no way victims of circumstance.

I hope you will use what is said in the following pages to become the master of your destiny, and not rely on the predictions that are given as mere fate but as valuable guidelines to use intelligently when life presents you with its certain challenges.

Neither the outside world, nor the ups and downs that occur in your life, should affect your innermost spirituality and self-confidence. Take control: look beyond your current challenges and use them as the building blocks of experience to create success and fulfilment in the coming year.

I believe you have the power to become great and shine your light for all to see. I hope your 2010 horoscope book will be a helpful guide and inspiration for you.

Warm regards, and may the stars shine brightly for you in 2010!

Your Astrologer,

Dadhichi Toth

Contents

The Aquarius Identity 11

Aquarius: A Snapshot 13

Star Sign Compatibility 35

2010: The Year Ahead 67

2010: Month By Month Predictions 81

January 83

February 88

March 93

April 98

May 103

June 109

July 114

August 119

September 124

October 129

November 134

December 138

2010: Astronumerology 143

2010: Your Daily Planner 171

AQUARIUS

The Aquarius Identity

As a single footstep will not make a path on the earth, so a single thought will not make a pathway in the mind. To make a deep physical path, we walk again and again. To make a deep mental path, we must think over and over the kind of thoughts we wish to dominate our lives.

—Henry David Thoreau

Aquarius: A Snapshot

Key Characteristics

Unconventional, distinctive, humanitarian, eccentric, outgoing, decisive, detached

Compatible Star Signs

Gemini, Libra, Sagittarius, Aries

Key Life Phrase

I progress

Life Goals

To lead others with integrity and instigate change

Platinum Assets

Unique intellectual skills, progressive attitude, true friend

Zodiac Totem

The Water Bearer

Zodiac Symbol

♒

Zodiac Facts

Eleventh sign of the zodiac; fixed, barren, masculine

Element

Air

Famous Aquarians

Chris Rock, Eartha Kitt, Edward Van Halen, Garth Brooks, Nick Nolte, Seth Green, Diane Lane, Oprah Winfrey, Tom Selleck, Gene Hackman, Phil Collins, Wolfgang Mozart, Prince Andrew, Paris Hilton, Charles Darwin, Abraham Lincoln, Jennifer Aniston, Joe Pesci, Natalie Imbruglia, Peter Gabriel, Lisa Marie Presley, Justin Timberlake

Aquarius: Your profile

There's nothing at all dull and boring about being an Aquarian. You're born under the progressive energies of the electric planet Uranus, which gives you a dose of cosmic current that supercharges your personality. You are popular, exciting and always individualistic in style.

Those who know you find you quirky but definitely loveable. And if you were to ask someone to give their description of you in a nutshell, it would be 'harmlessly mad'. You're loved everywhere you make your presence felt, but not always immediately. You like to size up the situation before 'throwing your hat in the ring', socially or personally. This makes you appear aloof, distant and possibly even a little bit snobbish in manner. Bad luck for those who don't give you the time to reveal your true Aquarian gifts!

They'll miss out on a truly unique experience being associated with you. You're self-sufficient and really prefer doing things in your own way, in your own good time. You never really enjoy treading anyone else's path, so you can sometimes feel alone in your life's journey, wondering why others don't understand your motivations.

Helping others comes naturally to you. Aquarius is called 'the sign of man'. This means you're always on the lookout to assist others, to make their lives easier in any way you can. You look to the welfare of the group rather than of the individual, and have a keen interest in humanity, the social sciences, politics and philosophy.

Anything that can be used as a tool for improving the world and society generally will be of interest to you. You seek to uplift yourself and others through wisdom and knowledge. You possess a progressive attitude, and at times you will confound your family and friends with concepts that seem to be 200 years ahead of their time!

Try keeping your outlandish ideas to yourself until you feel comfortable that others are ready to hear what you offer. And this goes for any advice you give to friends when they come to call on your assistance. What is perfectly correct in your estimation is scary to others because it's so new and revolutionary.

Speaking of revolution, many born under your sign of Aquarius have the natural urge to overthrow established values and traditions. This can make you appear dangerous to those who have a more conservative way of thinking and seeing things. In your workplace and society, don't be too forceful in rallying others to perform any sort of mutiny. It might cost you more than you expect because obviously the average person fears such a radical change so quickly.

You are a great communicator, with fresh new perspectives. You analyse well and draw unique conclusions because of your brilliant thinking. You're valued for your clear and precise expression, and always welcomed in a social scenario that requires a little bit of zest and energy.

Uranus is your planetary ruler and it is notorious for causing unsettling events in your life. Unexpected, even shocking circumstances occur from time to time. But they will be welcomed by you because you hate monotonous routine and realise that any sort of mental or spiritual growth is not possible without change.

You are a friend to everyone and extend yourself to those who request your help, whether they are high or low in position. It doesn't matter if it's a king or a beggar who approaches you because you have the wonderful ability to treat all people as equals. You're certainly not a 'high brow' sort of person.

Your love of people is genuine and you are loyal to your friends and family. This brings with it a great deal of respect for you.

You're unconventional in the way you live your life, and if others do decide to join with you in this journey, they should be prepared for some thrills and spills.

Three classes of Aquarius

If you're an Aquarian born between the 21st and the 31st of January, you are a particularly clever sort of Aquarian with an inventive and research-orientated personality. You also love technology and want to have the latest mobile phones, computers or other gadgets at hand that can make your life more comfortable. You're a great communicator and love to share your ideas with others.

You are particularly insightful if you're born between the 10th and 19th of February. You think on a larger scale than most people and have an expansive, universal attitude. You are the consummate learner and like to make friends who are as different as you. You will never stop studying or absorbing information to improve yourself and the world around you.

If you're born between the 1st and the 9th of February, you are a progressive type of individual who might not always make friends easily because you are so different in manner to them. You pride yourself on being unique, individualistic, and at times can be rather wilful in holding your ground.

A little flexibility will go a long way and bring you much more satisfaction in life, remember that.

Aquarius role model: Peter Gabriel

Peter Gabriel continues to shine his Aquarian talents through music. He was well known in the 1980s and '90s for his unique spin on music and now fosters Third World composition with a view to bringing the world and its cultures closer together. These aspirations perfectly reflect his and your Aquarian ideals.

Aquarius: The light side

You have a bubbly personality thanks to your ruling planet Uranus. Others are attracted to you because of your transparent, clear and fun-loving ways. You make a strong impression on people once they're able to get beyond the initial cool exterior you project as a means of protecting your inner self.

The higher side of Aquarius is attracted to charitable, social and humanitarian works. You have a selflessness that can be used to uplift the world, which is probably your greatest asset in life.

You're able to help others in their time of need and, because you are sincere and straight up and down in the way you deal with them, you are held in high esteem by most who know you.

Finally, impartiality is one of your other greatest traits, making you a fair judge when it comes to dealing with the world on a day-to-day basis. You can never be accused of bias.

Aquarius: The shadow side

In your desire to change the world, to think differently and push forward your progressive ideas, you can tend to be somewhat wilful and stubborn with it. Although you have an impartial view of the world and are unbiased in your judgements, there are times when your opinions leave very little room for others to have their say, even sideways. You must be careful not to let this wilfulness detract from your generally good relationship with people.

Unfortunately you love spontaneity to such an extent that you're likely to drop everything at a moment's notice and quickly change direction in life. If you're independent, without others relying on you, this is quite okay. But if you are in a relationship where someone else is depending on you, it can become quite frightening for them, for example, when you decide to jump on a plane and go to Borneo to live with the gorillas to study their mating habits.

Try to make some concessions for others by planning some time ahead when making your world-shattering decisions that can impact on them.

Aquarius woman

It's women like you, Aquarius, that spearhead change in the world. You may not be an icon as such, a famous person strutting the world's stage, but in your own way, within your own circle of influence, you will create change simply by being who you are.

Aquarian women are unique in every respect. You are a liberated, 21st century person who values intelligent change as a means of personal growth and wisdom. Wherever you can you endeavour to act as a catalyst for meaningful evolution and progress, both individually, within your family, and socially as well.

You're not the type of woman that an 'ordinary' person finds easy to deal with because you constantly challenge mediocrity by pushing others to be their best and shine their talents to the world, just like you do. Not many will pass the test in their association with you; but this doesn't matter because you'll keep trying to push them forward.

You are creative, especially intellectually, and never cease to question the reason why things are the way they are. You enjoy mental stimulation and like to learn. Reading and studying fascinate you. Some Aquarian women are bookworms. You inherently understand that knowledge is power.

Apart from being creative people themselves, Aquarian women have the knack of being able to inspire others to creative action as well. You don't feel comfortable unless you are surrounded by people who have a mission in life, too, and are able to artistically, creatively express themselves in a similar fashion.

Your intellectual pursuits are quite eclectic and you therefore need to communicate and befriend others who are able to appreciate diverse interests. This makes you truly feel alive.

Until someone truly gets to understand who you are, they may never fully realise the depth of your emotions and sensitivity. Although I have harped on about just how intellectual and communicative you are as a person, it is important to realise that the Aquarian woman is indeed a soft, loving and affectionate individual when given the opportunity to express this side of her character. Perhaps her intellectual leanings are the way an Aquarian protects her deeply-running feelings.

In your social networks you surround yourself with those who have intelligence as well. You respect good communication and like working with others to come up with novel solutions for all manner of problems.

You are born under a fixed air sign, which makes you stubborn, determined to some extent and also argumentative, especially if discussions centre on topics you are familiar with or in which you are an expert.

Some Aquarian women are over-reactive and hypersensitive, which creates troubles in their relationships. You will need to be a little more thick-skinned to overcome such traits. However, being so sensitive does have an upside. You are naturally intuitive and can sense when something is not right.

You use this psychic ability quite readily to solve your practical and relationship problems. Being as finely tuned as you are, I can only recommend that you trust this power you have and not rely too much on the mental side of your personality. At the end of the day, a balance between both of these extraordinary Aquarian traits would be ideal.

Overall, however, I must say that the Aquarian woman is a valuable asset to our world, and will be appreciated for her contribution in every aspect of life.

Aquarius man

An Aquarian man is somewhat of an anomaly, because he's not easy to understand. If you were born under the sign of Aquarius, you may initially be dismissed as being a little too aloof or snobbish in manner. But this tough exterior you exhibit to the outside world actually hides a warm, sensitive and caring individual. If others would only take a moment or two to look beneath the surface, they'll be in for a very pleasant surprise.

'Freedom' and 'progress' are your key words and, as an Aquarian male, you hate any sort of constraint, either by friends, by family or, would you believe, by society. This is why you need to be careful in the way you buck authority and 'the system', particularly in your work and more conventional relationships. You are likely to say and do things that are shocking and could get others offside. But you'd rather risk being chastised than curtail your free flow of expression concerning what you believe in.

Aquarian men are original and your ruling planet Uranus gives you adequate opportunity to express your unique ideas. Apart from the intellectual brilliance that you often display, you may also find yourself getting flashes of intuition that make you somewhat of a psychic individual as well. Incidentally, the sign of Aquarius does have a strong rulership over such things as astrology, new age topics and other forms of psychic or paranormal activity. You'd be great at this sort of stuff.

You have an intellectual approach to life and prefer to think things through rather than following blindly. You're a non-conformist and like to reason the whys and wherefores. Typical conventional thinking is frustrating for you; but more than the actual thoughts themselves are the systems of thought that you will rebel against. You are the type of man who likes to set in motion new methodologies and systems to streamline life and play your part in the process of progress.

Aquarian men can be stubborn sometimes and usually you have a good reason to be. You are very well studied on your topic of interest and usually have an arsenal of facts and figures to back up your arguments.

You're also an adventurous type of character, enjoying travel for the sake of furthering and expanding your horizons intellectually and culturally.

You can be a great leader because of your far-reaching vision and ability to inspire and motivate others. Living up to this responsibility, however, means taking into account the different stages of life that each of us is at, and not assuming that everyone can progress as quickly as you do. This basically means you must also respect the societal norms to become successful yourself.

Although you are cool in temperament, you are rather wilful and reactive when you want to be. Balancing your feelings will play an important part in maintaining good health and a peaceful mind. The Aquarian male is cut out for a special future, but you must also be patient and balanced in trying to attain these very high-reaching goals.

Aquarius child

Being the parent of an Aquarian child can get rather frustrating at times, because they just won't do things the way others expect them to do it. The child of Aquarius is a little dynamo, with a powerful intellectual capacity and a never-ending curiosity to understand everything.

They have a unique temperament, and unless you spend adequate time with them, their complicated psychological make-up may baffle you at times. Communication will always be the secret to understanding where they're coming from.

Don't try to force your Aquarian child to do anything, because force won't work. Actually, the more you push them in a certain direction, the more they will resist you, trying to move in the opposite direction. This is because they have such a strong sense of individuality that they don't want to feel as though they're like everyone else. The trick of getting them onside is to respect them for their original ways but try to help them fit in with the group at the same time.

Most children love playing games of some sort, but your Aquarian child has a very strategic and sharp mind so physical sports may not be ideal for them. Give them unusual or intellectual games and puzzles to help challenge them, and this will be an excellent way for them to develop their curious abilities. Tennis, golf, climbing and hiking may also be wonderful ways to satisfy their need for sport and intellectual strategy.

Because your Aquarian child likes to explore and invent, you'll find them tinkering with all manner of mechanical and electrical equipment. But don't forget, 'curiosity killed the cat', so you should always pay special attention to what your Aquarian child is doing to prevent them harming themselves. For example, they could fiddle with a power point to see exactly what electricity feels like!

Aquarian children are adventurous types, so they need lots of walking and also rest to help balance their highly strung nerves. Being ruled by the planet Uranus makes them prone to surges of electrical and nervous energy, which can be damaging, especially if they don't eat or sleep enough.

Continually being challenged is important for the young Aquarius so they can feel a sense of achievement. You may need to look at alternative forms of education to give them the stimulation and challenge they require.

Romance, love and marriage

You're in for a rude shock if you think a relationship with an Aquarian is going to be the typical 'boy meets girl' scenario: ring on finger, walk up the aisle, have children and live happily ever after. It will be anything but that!

An Aquarian has a very strong sense of self and wants to impress their unique personality on their relationships indelibly and, in particular, their romantic and marital connections. Aquarians generally have very powerful willpower and extremely strong opinions. But their opinions are not born of a second-hand knowledge or hand-me-down ideas. They are unique in their way of looking at things and drawing their own conclusions in life.

You'll understand exactly what I'm saying when you look back over your life to see just how wonderfully you've synthesised the experiences that have come your way, to make your own brand of philosophy and a lifestyle that fits in with who you are. This is a rather amazing thing; I could even call it magical, because you are able to transform the most mundane of experiences into something quite extraordinary.

This is what makes it hard for others to grasp who you really are in your inner self. And you don't always reveal this to everyone. Only a lucky few will be able to get close enough to you, Aquarius. This is why you tend to use different masks on different occasions to keep people at arm's length until you thoroughly understand them.

Aquarians have an individualistic view on life and in many cases don't settle down till they've exhausted their search for someone unique and special. You will want to explore the possibilities that are available to you in life, which could make you cross the oceans far and wide in your search for someone who matches your ideals. It's only when you've exhausted your search for the right person (whether you find them or not) that you're likely to settle down and be a little more content with what some would consider a normal, day-to-day relationship.

Because freedom is at the core of your personality, a relationship needs to afford you the opportunity to continue to discover who you are; therefore, marriage to an Aquarian is in itself a rather unusual lifestyle. If you're reading this and you're attached to an Aquarian, you'll know what I mean when you see them demanding that you step back and not interfere with their personal agendas to continue to explore themselves.

Aquarians, either male or female, can never be controlled. Controlling them would be a mistake because they need equality, at least, or preferably to be the one dominating the way in which the relationship proceeds.

Aquarians need excitement, change, an intense range of variety and emotional goals to make them feel fulfilled in a relationship. If you are an Aquarian and looking for love, you might understand me when I say that you set the standard very high and therefore may not find your soulmate as quickly as others do.

In love, you expect your partner to support some of your social and global desires. To you, love is not simply a matter of sex and emotional comfort. You'd like to believe that you can work with your partner towards a greater good, which is why Aquarius is considered the 'new age' sign, always concerned with social and communal issues. If you can find someone who empathises with these idealistic aspirations, then you'll be completely fulfilled in your search for the perfect love.

Sexually, you like the idea of exploring new avenues, and may even be a little unconventional in expecting your partner to give you the freedom to explore friendships outside your primary commitment. This may be going a little bit far, but if you're fortunate enough to find someone who will cut you that much slack, good luck to you.

Health, wellbeing and diet

The element of air rules your birth sign of Aquarius, so your thinking processes, your nervous system and even the brain and spinal fluid come under the rulership of your sign.

When this is the case, there are certain parts of your body, as mentioned above, that may be constitutionally weak. It's important for you to pay special attention towards keeping these organs healthy and feeding them with the appropriate nutrition to make them strong over time.

Because you have an ambitious and intense streak about your personality, you tend to overwork and therefore your thinking and nervous system come under excessive strain. One of the easiest ways to overcome such problems is to sleep more and not overwork your weary nerves. It's important to give yourself special time to relax, meditate and resuscitate.

Another portion of the human body ruled by Aquarius is the lower part of the body, including the ankles. The shins may also be subject to problems and injuries. Celery is a wonderful food to strengthen the bones and you may include it in some sort of vegetable juice intake. Carrots, apples, lemons and celery mixed together make a delicious and healthy drink. You should try it.

Being an air sign means you like talking; but when you eat, focus on your eating rather than talking to others. This will assist in digestion and help you absorb more nutrients.

Some Aquarians are deficient in B, C and K vitamins. Therefore, taking a multivitamin supplement can help rebuild your nerve and skin tissue and also make your bones much stronger.

I always recommend soy bean products and, for Aquarians, these along with bean sprouts and other high-protein foods such as lean meats, egg and wheatgerm will provide you with a wonderful source of these vitamins.

Many Aquarians, being ruled by new age energies, will also—at least at some time in their lives—experiment with macrobiotic and other vegetarian food regimes. No harm in trying but you should always listen to your body's responses and, if in doubt, consult your health physician, your doctor or your naturopath.

Other fruits and vegetables useful for the Aquarian are broccoli, lettuce, spinach, potatoes, mandarins, mangoes and other low-fat sources of protein such as cheese and milk or yoghurt.

Uranus, your ruling planet, is very abrupt in nature, so you should avoid eating when you are angry, over-emotional or tired. This will give your digestive system a chance to recuperate.

Work

Because you're so ambitious and want to change the world, work is a natural fit for the Aquarian. Money is important to you but not as important as creating some sort of noble and life-changing work. You like mental challenges and jobs that are stimulating to you and others.

Irrespective of the work you choose, you need it to be in a setting where you can deal with others and express your ideas, thereby making notable contributions to the immediate work group and to society at large.

You need a harmonious place in which to do your best work. If you are surrounded by like-minded people who support you in trying out your new ideas, then all the better; your work will be excellent. But you do need people who are open-minded enough to give you a chance to explore your ingenuity. You tend to bounce your great ideas off other people because this triggers even more dynamic intellectual energy in your professional initiatives.

If you are hindered in expressing your novel and unique concepts, this will frustrate you and the power of Uranus in its negative attributes can be rather frightening. Imagine an electrical storm in the office with thunder, lightning and a hurricane thrown in for good measure. That can describe the very strong reaction of an Aquarian who is hampered in their objectives.

Because communication is one of your strongest fortes, teaching, sales and other marketing avenues are perfect for an Aquarian's professional satisfaction. And, as well, because you have an intuitive understanding, you could also work in the new age arts such as astrology, clairvoyance, palmistry or numerology.

Key to karma, spirituality and emotional balance

The words 'I progress' make up the key phrase for those of you born under Aquarius. Therefore, your uninhibited mind is constantly working to break the limits of the current conditions in life for yourself and others. You may try a little too hard; therefore, you may need to learn the art of relaxation and meditation to help you get to your goal in one piece.

First and foremost, you need to balance progressive ideas with what traditional and conservative society deems to be necessary. Commitment is another area that needs to be worked on by you, Aquarius. In your relationships, you must never promise your heart to anyone when in fact you're not quite prepared to settle down. Learning to be satisfied with where you are and with whom you are is one of the big spiritual lessons for you.

Because your nervous system can be a little strung out at times, you are especially advised to meditate on Wednesdays, Fridays and Saturdays so that you can soothe your emotions and nerves and further expand your awareness, which will lead to health and personal fulfilment.

Your lucky days

Your luckiest days are Friday, Saturday and Wednesday, being ruled by the planets that are most friendly to you.

Your lucky numbers

Explore the value of these following lucky numbers:

6, 15, 24, 33, 42, 51

5, 14, 23, 32, 41, 50

4, 13, 22, 31, 40, 49

Your destiny years

Your most important years are 4, 13, 22, 31, 40, 49, 58, 67, 76 and 85.

AQUARIUS

Star Sign Compatibility

They say love is blind ... and marriage is an institution. Well, I'm not ready for an institution for the blind just yet.

—Mae West

Romantic compatibility

How compatible are you with your current partner, lover or friend? Did you know that astrology can reveal a whole new level of understanding between people simply by looking at their star sign and that of their partner? In this chapter I'd like to share some special insights that will help you better appreciate your strengths and challenges using Sun sign compatibility.

The Sun reflects your drive, willpower and personality. The essential qualities of two star signs blend like two pure colours, producing an entirely new colour. Relationships, similarly, produce their own emotional colours when two people interact. The following is a general guide to your romantic prospects with others and how, by knowing the astrological 'colour' of each other, the art of love can help you create a masterpiece.

When reading the following I ask you to remember that no two star signs are ever *totally* incompatible. With effort and compromise, even the most 'difficult' astrological matches can work. Don't close your mind to the full range of life's possibilities! Learning about each other and ourselves is the most important facet of astrology.

Quick-reference guide: Horoscope compatibility between signs (percentage)

	Aries	Taurus	Gemini	Cancer	Leo	Virgo	Libra	Scorpio	Sagittarius	Capricorn	Aquarius	Pisces
Aries	60	65	65	65	90	45	70	80	90	50	55	65
Taurus	60	70	70	80	70	90	75	85	50	95	80	85
Gemini	70	70	75	60	80	75	90	60	75	50	90	50
Cancer	65	80	60	75	70	75	60	95	55	45	70	90
Leo	90	70	80	70	85	75	65	75	95	45	70	75
Virgo	45	90	75	75	75	70	80	85	70	95	50	70
Libra	70	75	90	60	65	80	80	85	80	85	95	50
Scorpio	80	85	60	95	75	85	85	90	80	65	60	95
Sagittarius	90	50	75	55	95	70	80	85	85	55	60	75
Capricorn	50	95	50	45	45	95	85	65	55	85	70	85
Aquarius	55	80	90	70	70	50	95	60	60	70	80	55
Pisces	65	85	50	90	75	70	50	95	75	85	55	80

Each star sign combination is followed by the elements of those star signs and the result of their combining. For instance, Aries is a fire sign and Aquarius is an air sign and this combination produces a lot of 'hot air'. Air feeds fire and fire warms air. In fact, fire requires air. However, not all air and fire combinations work. I have included information about the different birth periods within each star sign and this will throw even more light on your prospects for a fulfilling love life with any star sign you choose.

Good luck in your search for love, and may the stars shine upon you in 2010!

Compatibility quick-reference guide

Each of the twelve star signs has a greater or lesser affinity with one another. The quick-reference guide will show you who's hot and who's not so hot as far as your relationships are concerned.

AQUARIUS + ARIES

Air + Fire = Hot Air

Aquarius and Aries are not particularly well suited. The fiery Aries may eventually annoy you with their continual 'I'm right' attitude, even when you know full well they aren't. You are always well-armed with the facts, cool as a cucumber under siege, and somewhat bemused by Aries' intense attacks. But you won't stand for it for too long and will weary of the Arian ego.

There's quite a bit of intellectual stimulation for you by Aries and you like their dynamic approach to life. In some ways you live in a similar fashion, but more than likely are less impulsive in your decisions.

Your sign of Aquarius happens to fall in the zone of friendship for Aries, so your time together will fan the flames of the Arian fire and elevate your relationship to one of passion. Friendship is a good basis for deepening your sexual and intimate appetites.

As an 'item' you'll be surprised at the types of people you'll meet through your mutual association. This combination can sometimes be very wacky and high-powered socially.

You are quite determined to change things and always look to the greater good for all concerned, whereas Aries is a little more self-absorbed and less humanitarian in approach.

Uranus and Mars, your respective rulers, are explosive together! Just because you don't always see eye to eye on everything doesn't mean you're not excited by each other. You are. In fact, your elements, air and fire, result in an explosive combination.

You are likely to want mutual mobility, excitement and experiences. But you do need to define your mission as a couple if you go against the general consensus and try to make a go of it.

You might have problems temperamentally with Aries born between the 21st and the 30th of March. This is in particular a very volatile mix due to the fiery energies of Aries. Both of you will have to be moderate and you, in particular, be sensitive in the way you voice your opinions to your Aries because they can be very reactive to criticism.

There is one group of Aries, those born between the 31st of March and the 10th of April, who are probably a little more compatible with you than the rest. Leo has a strong influence over them, and Leo, being your sign of marriage, indicates there's quite a bit of attraction between you. It could indeed be a karmic connection that you find hard to pass by. You could have a powerful relationship with these individuals.

With Aries born between the 11th and the 20th of April you can expect a reasonably good relationship. They have the strong flavours of Jupiter and Mars in their personalities and this makes them generous and open-minded. You'll find much mutual respect in their company. They're friendly and enjoy socialising so you can have a lot of fun with these characters.

AQUARIUS + TAURUS

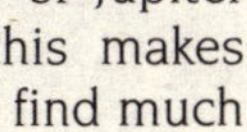

Air + Earth = Dust

Taurus is probably a little more stubborn than Aquarius and I'd suggest you discover this sooner rather than later. Taurus digs in its heels and doesn't let go. You, in your own way, are also inflexible but do know when change is absolutely necessary.

Telling Taurus how and when to do things is risky for this relationship, remember that. Patience will be the essential quality you must exhibit if you want to move things forward together.

In life generally Taurus is quite conventional. But you're progressive and you'll deliberately try to push them out of their comfort zone. Okay, do that, but this will be a perilous experiment on your part, so be warned! You'll need to be prepared for a violent reaction when the Taurean bull decides to charge. Put away any red flags for now.

You could make Taurus feel somewhat insecure. Money and material things are important to them. But if you also happen to like a comfortable lifestyle and can prove you will support them in this goal, then they'll love you to death.

Taurus is slow off the mark sexually but your patience with them will be more than rewarded if you work to satisfy their deep inner emotional needs. Share your exciting love-making techniques with them and this will unlock their sensual, Venusian energies. They do have a lot to offer you in this regard.

If you join hands with a Taurean born between the 21st and the 29th of April, Venus has a strong sway over their lives and it means they are more suited to you than most others born under this sign. A romantic association with them will be mutually satisfying. They also seem to understand just what you need emotionally and mentally and will do their best to fulfil you. They are extremely loyal individuals.

With Taureans born between the 30th of April and the 10th of May, expect a stubborn streak to be part of their character. Nevertheless you'll still want to spend time with them and have a natural attraction towards these bulls. You must not try to argue with their opinions and must go along for the ride until you gently try to coax them into looking at alternatives. This will work for you.

A more intensely inflexible group of Taureans is born between the 11th and the 21st of May. With these characters you'll become frustrated, especially if you're a more progressive and forward-thinking character yourself. This is really not a great match because you like to change the status quo, whereas they like to keep it the same.

AQUARIUS + GEMINI

Air + Air = Wind

Aquarius is an air element, and so is Gemini. Essentially star signs of the same element do have a lot going for them if they fall in love with each other.

Air is light, intellectual and in perpetual motion. These qualities refer particularly to Gemini in that they are always on the go, mentally curious and extremely talkative.

You like these qualities and the two of you automatically plug into each other's minds and hearts. This is definitely a soul connection and should be honoured as such. Finding such a soulmate is rare, which is why the two of you score highly in the compatibility arena.

There is a danger that, Aquarius being ruled by Uranus, the unpredictable planet, and Gemini by Mercury, the flighty and scattered communication planet, the two of you will need to set some boundaries by which to live and determine your lifestyles. Too much change, excessive communication and not enough 'me time' for either of you will certainly damage the relationship over time.

Fortunately you are both caring–sharing individuals and this is why your love should grow and strengthen in future. Gemini does need some gentle direction and if anyone is going to do it, Aquarius can.

Your sexual relationship is also dynamic, with a childlike innocence infusing your intimate moments. Cherish and nurture each other because this truly is a great match. The strength in your intimacy with each other will rest upon your strong understanding as communicators—and great talkers you are.

You'll spend many satisfying hours sharing your earnest thoughts, ideas and wild imaginations. Naturally, the way you express your ideas will be slightly different to each other. Gemini's very happy to jump from one topic to another, like a butterfly. This often lacks the depth and continuity that you'd prefer.

You have a more focused concentration and like to savour the facts rather than moving on to new themes. Gemini will learn that you insist on a focused way of dealing with people. However, Gemini does possess versatility in the way they speak and you will learn a lot from each other.

Your best strength with Geminis born between the 22nd of May and the 1st of June is your mutual communication. There's a creative power that arises when the two of you get together, which means that this relationship is a great working one in addition to being romantically very well matched.

You have a great connection with Geminis born between the 2nd and the 12th of June. You feel as if your life is transformed by your association with them, and before you know it, your personality may also be somewhat transformed. You can be great friends as well as enjoying many sexual experiences together. This is a great combination.

You fit naturally, temperamentally, with Geminis born between the 13th and the 21st of June. There's an immediate attraction and your compatibility won't be questioned by either of you. This is one of those rare, karmic relationships that should be considered a universal gift.

AQUARIUS + CANCER

Air + Water = Rain

Sensitive Cancer operates from a purely emotional level and, although you admire this, generally you prefer a little more head than heart.

Cancer is also conventional in many respects, whereas you like to jump to the future, leapfrogging the obstacles of stuffy thinking and cultural bias.

However, try not to equate the home-loving Cancer with stuffy, traditional constraints or you might just miss the point of a 'real-ationship' with watery Cancer.

First thing's first, though. Unless you offer Cancer security, love and understanding by way of feeling and listening, then forget it! Your partnership won't make it to first base. As an Aquarian you need to explore the highways and byways of life before making any firm commitment. If the Cancerian you happen to be thinking of has a conservative or traditional nature, they might be waiting an awfully long time to have their personal needs satisfied by you. You'll have to be honest and let them know that there's still too much for you to explore to be tied down.

And another thing: you'll need to be extremely adaptable when dealing with their rather extreme mood swings. Yes, Cancer is one of the most emotional of the star signs and you'll need to resonate with these fluctuating mental and emotional states. These moods are very strongly related to Cancer's ruler, the Moon. Unless you're able to get into the swing of this, your relationship will fail to launch.

You don't tend to be a good fit sexually, either.

Your freedom-loving ways and exploratory views are extreme to Cancer, to say the least. They need you to be exclusively theirs and therefore the big, million-dollar question is: 'Are you up for this sacrifice?'

When speaking about these intense mood swings, Cancerians born between the 22nd of June and the 3rd of July are a case in point. And you'll notice that the Moon does dominate their day-to-day behaviour. Expect an emotional roller-coaster ride to exasperate your cool, intellectual temperament.

With Cancers born between the 4th and the 13th of July you'll be attracted to their rather quirky personalities. Spend time getting to know them because they're not particularly your best match. But, showing them a little extra interest could spark a mutual flame that can develop into a more fulfilling relationship for the two of you.

You can expect a reasonably good friendship to occur between you and those Cancers born between the 14th and the 23rd of July. You feel pretty comfortable when you're in their company and socially this is not a bad match.

AQUARIUS + LEO

Air + Fire = Hot Air

Aquarius and Leo are opposites, which is good. Air and fire work well together, too; sometimes so well that this combination can be quite volatile. As the heading says, air plus fire equals explosion!

Your ruling planets are not the best of friends and, furthermore, Leo will constantly challenge you for the limelight. On the one hand, you like their outgoing, warm and vibrant personalities, but also find yourself competing for attention at times. This could create tension between what should otherwise be a good relationship.

Leo is naturally bright and attractive to everyone. They don't have to prove their intellectual abilities like you do. They are ruled by the Sun so their very presence makes others stand to attention when they walk into a room.

Some Leos are more conservative than you think. On the other hand, you're very forward thinking and even border on having an impertinent outlook on life. You might ask yourself if there's any merit in this relationship? Well, yes. You could find yourselves attracted to each other.

You're always abrupt or sudden in the way you do things. Marriage between an Aquarius and Leo also is likely to be the same. You might just fall in love before you realise it. There's a natural attraction between Aquarius and Leo, therefore marriage or at least a serious relationship between you might be inevitable once you meet.

You're both fixed signs and will often disagree on many topics. You may well respect each other, but you are incredibly different. You mustn't let your egos dominate your love life. So, who will be the hero in this match: you, Aquarius? This tension between you will act as fuel for the passion of your physical love. Therefore, when all is said and done, you'll more than likely still enjoy making love even though underneath all this there will be considerable tension and ego clashes.

You're naturally attracted to Leos born between the 24th of July and the 4th of August. These characters have huge amounts of confidence and this attracts you, showing promise for a long-term relationship with them. You're both keen to understand the deeper aspects of human nature so you'll want to explore each other's personalities and find ways of balancing the tensions mentioned earlier.

The group of Leos born between the 5th and 14th of August make excellent friends. As long as you can enjoy being friends with them without trying to hold onto them, they'll hang around for the long term. Money can be made by both of you as a team due to past good karma.

Those Leos born between the 15th and the 23rd of August are ruled by fiery Mars, which will create some upheavals for you both if you choose to walk the path of love with them. There can be disputes and, although you could experience some good times with them, the bickering might end up eroding what love you have for each other.

AQUARIUS + VIRGO

Air + Earth = Dust

Virgo is one of the most precise and intellectually curious of the zodiac signs, and you'll be immediately drawn to this quality in them. But take note, Aquarius: Virgos are also highly critical individuals and they will challenge your authority on almost everything you believe in. You thought you had most things in the bag, didn't you? Well, that may not be the case once you start dating a Virgo.

If your ego is humble enough, you can learn a lot from Virgo, and vice versa. You must put aside your egos and truly listen to each other's viewpoints to learn the lessons of the Aquarius–Virgo match.

There is a crossover, though, because both of you are interested in doing something to improve the world. Virgo has a more personal approach to serving others whereas you, Aquarius, are more community, society or even globally focused. You could work together to improve the world, or may possibly meet in some work-related activity that brings you together.

You must remember that Virgo is not just tidy and meticulous in their environment; they are methodical thinkers as well. This could drive you crazy because you like to break the rules from time to time, whereas Virgo will never let you do that without eternally questioning your motives.

Many lessons lie in store for you with Virgo,

especially in areas of sex and intimacy. Helping Virgos to release their tension, to relax their uptight, prudish views, could become a mission for you. That's okay, as long as it's not a lifelong one.

You have much in common with Virgo, but it's not always immediately obvious. They see a lot of themselves in your caring and collective orientation. There are some differences between you as well, though. For example, you aren't as preoccupied with the nitty gritty of helping others, like Virgo is. You're a 'big picture' person and concerned about contributing to the community and the world as a whole. Nevertheless, your noble ideas do attract Virgo and this is a good basis for friendship, if not a romantic relationship.

Virgos born between the 24th of August and the 2nd of September are reasonably well matched with you because they have good sexual compatibility. These are the liberated Virgos, and therefore you'll enjoy their company and have a better chance of developing not only your sexual prowess with them but also your intellectual ideas. They're not quite as judgemental as your typical Virgo.

There's also a reasonable compatibility with Virgos born between the 3rd and the 12th of September. They have a similar way of thinking, which suits you, and therefore your discussions could be quite riveting and stimulating to each other.

Those Virgos born between the 13th and the 23rd of September are really quite spiritual in nature. Initially you might not feel they are ideally suited to you for the long term. Think again because these people are probably your best partners since Venus has a strong rulership over them and this is one of the best planets for Aquarius.

AQUARIUS + LIBRA

Air + Air = Wind

As mentioned earlier, two air signs are a no-brainer when it comes to a combination of love and romance. You'll like each other from the word go, because you each feel so at ease in the company of the other.

If you're an Aquarian, Libra will be your knight in shining armour, or princess, coming to the rescue. They'll know just how to calm you down, and make you feel secure on all levels of your being. After all, they are ruled by Venus, the goddess of love.

You'll find Libra to be suave, engaging, graceful and sociable, and you'll be proud to be loved by them. But, they need as much rope as you can give them to hang themselves, socially. They love to be free and engage friends, so give them ample space. Tell them you love them as many times as possible, communicate your feelings to them, and you'll win them over in a flash. They'll be yours for keeps.

Together you'll be a wonderful couple, very much in tune, with your social lives dominating your affairs. There's also a strong karmic bond between you, which will bring with it many new lessons.

Either good or bad, these will be able to be dealt with together.

Both of you are incorrigible flirts, but this will work positively to keep you both on your toes and very much sexually attracted to each other. As well, both of you have progressive views about love and marriage, but Libra is probably less vocal about being seriously 'committed' to 'non-commitment' than you are. Some Aquarians still subscribe to the hippy notion of free love and freedom in their most intimate relationships. You may both be interested in exploring this aspect of your relationships.

Libra may well indulge in some harmless flirtations, but that's a far cry from your avant-garde attitude, which you want to push to the limits. You want to investigate the possibilities of freedom in intimacy. Perhaps the two of you need to develop this relationship on the basis of a casual arrangement before you permanently commit to a serious affair. Once you've satisfied your individual needs you'll have much more going for you. With that out of the way, a more traditional commitment will be appropriate.

In coming together with a Libran born between the 24th of September and the 3rd of October, you can expect this relationship to transform the two of you. Mutual inspiration will cause you to aim high and both do your best to achieve great successes, individually and as a couple.

There are strong karmic connections with Librans born between the 4th and the 13th of October. You may feel that there's been some past-life association with these people; but even if you don't, the chemistry together will be great. This closeness will be experienced immediately and should become a great foundation for a durable partnership.

There's a strong mutual attachment between you and Librans born between the 14th and the 23rd of October, but the relationship may stall from time to time. You're great friends, enjoy each other's company and have many common interests but, because you're such an independent person, a long-term commitment might be a fairly big obstacle for you.

AQUARIUS + SCORPIO

Air + Water = Rain

Although most astrology books would try to convince you that a relationship between Aquarius and Scorpio is not particularly compatible, the fact is these signs are attracted to each other, and powerfully, too. This has been my experience in the past.

While a successful relationship cannot be assured, something will draw you together and you just won't be able to resist the temptation to get closer to each other. Aquarius is fascinated by Scorpio, and some deep, metaphysical intuition of theirs will intrigue you. Likewise, that sharp intellectual air quality of yours is a turn on for Scorpio because they love to think, and think deeply.

Generally, Scorpio is mysterious and secretive to a large extent. But earlier-born Scorpios do tend to be more verbal than classical astrologers suggest. This is therefore a great combination for sharing ideas, communication and spiritual connectedness. You highly respect each other's intelligence.

You're both able to complete projects and certainly aren't afraid of challenges. In a relationship, these abilities are essential ingredients that guarantee the long-term viability of your feelings. At least you both have the same doggedness needed to make this relationship work. Just don't let your obstinate opinions get in the way of true love. Learn to adjust to each other.

Aquarius and Scorpio are both determined and ambitious, but you need to make sure that you're 'on the same page' before heading off into the future together. Are you following the same star? Using the same compass? Double-check yourselves, to be safe. Otherwise you could end up in completely different places. Anticipate what you want in life, especially where love, romance and marriage are concerned.

This relationship is complex and demanding. You are both very opinionated and will try to convert the other to your own belief systems. 'Live and let live', I say. This is an essential philosophy for the Aquarian–Scorpion match. Scorpio will stimulate your physical passions and this might catch you off guard. They are, after all, masters of the sexual realm.

You have reasonably good commercial and business opportunities to develop with Scorpios born between the 24th of October and the 2nd of November. It's probably better to maintain the relationship on that basis. Remember the old adage that you should 'never mix business with pleasure'? You should be clear on your financial dealings with a Scorpio because there are some indications that this could jeopardise your friendship.

Scorpios born between the 3rd and the 12th of November are reasonably good partners for you. You like their intensity and the passion they bring to the relationship; although you sometimes wish they were a little more light-hearted and could express the softer side of their nature more often.

If you like a challenge, there is a group of complex Scorpions born between the 13th and the 22nd of November. This could be a rather destructive relationship. Nevertheless, you'll still learn much about each other and this is what could propel you both forward, at least for a little while.

AQUARIUS + SAGITTARIUS

Air + Fire = Hot Air

The bonds of friendship are quite strong between Aquarius and Sagittarius. Your zodiac elements of air and fire are agreeable, and this is a two-way street in terms of communication, sexuality and social interaction. If, as they say, 'it takes two to tango', then Aquarius and Sagittarius look set to spend a lot of time dancing together. Air feeds fire, and fire warms air. In short, you're very compatible as a couple.

Sagittarius has a philosophical yet free spirit, which in some ways is much like yours. They are habitual travellers, explorers, and a friend to all. You so much admire this in them. You'd even be prepared to forsake everything at the drop of a hat to escape with them on an expedition of a lifetime. Yes, a love affair between Aquarius and Sagittarius could be described just like this: an expedition into the unknown.

However, there are some differences I should point out. You have a more calculative approach to life, being an intellectual air sign, and Sagittarius is more spontaneous, relying on the need of the moment to make their decisions. You could find it difficult to reconcile these differences in your overall lifestyles, but will certainly enjoy them immensely when being together between the sheets.

As an Aquarian you are very methodical in most of the things you attempt to do and also have a strong opinion that change is essential for growth. And, yes, Sagittarius also appreciates capability and change; however, the types of changes we're talking about in your case are very radical and sometimes occur without any notice. This might throw Sagittarius out of kilter, even though they can be both inhibited and spontaneous, much like you. Perhaps not quite as much, though, would you agree?

The life of an Aquarian and Sagittarian will be dynamic and never dull or routine. You'll find yourselves absorbed in discussions about travel, social affairs and topics that no one else would dare to venture into. You'll entertain each other and can become the best of mates.

Sexually, I see a great deal of improvisation in the way you relate to each other. A progressive coming together of your minds creates a dynamic drive to your lovemaking. Burn, baby, burn! The intimate aspects of your relationship are high powered and exciting. You offer Sagittarius the thrills they're looking for. You're very pleasing to them.

Sagittarians are loving and emotional and will help you get more in tune with your heart rather than your head. They will turn you on by helping you switch off mentally, if you know what I mean. There are times when you are particularly highly strung and when this happens you need a Sagittarius by your side.

Sagittarians born between the 23rd of November and the 1st of December are wonderful friends for you. And it's quite likely that individuals born in this period could even be categorised as soulmates. They are a special breed and you love them.

You also can expect a wonderfully intimate time with Sagittarians born between the 2nd and the 11th of December. Your sexual energy together burns brightly. However, there's also a provocative element to this relationship that would cause you to argue a lot. Therefore, this side of your relationship will need to be carefully monitored.

Sagittarians born between the 12th and the 22nd of December are leonine in their nature and this is excellent because this sign of the zodiac is opposite to yours. They are loyal and loving individuals who want a relationship that is going to be durable. Expect lots of fun, dramatic and entertaining times, as well as a partner who will support you through thick or thin.

AQUARIUS + CAPRICORN

Air + Earth = Dust

The story of Aquarius and Capricorn is an unusual one, oscillating between bouts of strained optimism and outright frustration. This is a relationship that requires considerable effort from both of you if it is going to work.

This is a very strange astrological recipe because, although you are both ruled by Saturn and thus have qualities in common, you, Aquarius, have the additional influence of Uranus. Saturn is steady and predictable, and this is the governing characteristic of your Capricorn counterpart. You're rather unpredictable in nature due to Uranus's influence.

Each of you will feel on edge in the other's company. The tension should be quite pronounced because your ruling planets are like chalk and cheese. And so are your elements of air and earth, which produces dust. Does it sometimes feel like you're in a dust storm in the Gobi Desert? That's what might be in store if you decide to be hitched to a Capricorn.

I'm not making too many concessions for your romantic attachment with Capricorn, am I? But do you want the truth, or do you simply want me to make you feel good? This just isn't a particularly solid astrological combination, I'm sorry.

Sure, you'll both work hard at keeping the passion alive until one day you realise that the serious, sober Capricorn is just way too grounded or stodgy for your liking. And then you'll wonder why you invested so much energy into them. Capricorn, of course, is always preoccupied with money and work. While you're investing time in them, they'll probably be working hard keeping an eye on their bank balances and career schedules, not understanding where all that Aquarian altruism is going to lead them.

You love change and variety in sexual matters and relationships generally. Capricorn finds it difficult (not impossible, though) to move beyond their traditional values and procedures. Are you prepared to wait around for long enough to make that deeper, idealistic connection with Capricorn? Probably not.

Those Capricorns born between the 23rd of December and the 1st of January offer you a wonderful opportunity for friendship. You'll appreciate this and, even though you're both quite different temperamentally, there are some resemblances between you that will attract you to each other. Remember to work on the positives and your similarities rather than any negatives and differences.

There are good omens and opportunities to create a long-term relationship with Capricorns born between the 2nd and the 10th of January. They may seem quite different to you on the surface, but deep down there's a strong point of connectedness between you. I'd say this relationship has something very sweet going for it.

Capricorn natives born between the 11th and the 20th of January will stimulate your emotions and therefore you can also feel somewhat connected to them, irrespective of what I've said about Capricorn generally. They have a nice blend of sensitivity and emotionalism as well as practical and financial sense. You might feel satisfied with Capricorns born in this period.

AQUARIUS + AQUARIUS

Air + Air = Wind

Not all of the same-element combinations are guaranteed a perfect ride to relationship bliss. Aquarius and Aquarius is a pair of star twins that will blast their way from milestone to milestone on the road of love, which could frazzle both of you in the end.

Your ruling planet Uranus takes no prisoners in this relationship; but if you wear bulletproof vests, the shrapnel from such an explosive arrangement might not penetrate to your hearts. This is a volatile, unpredictable match and, yes, I admit, it is also exciting.

There won't be too much emotional stability between this pair of fixed air signs because that fixity resonates on unstable ground. Aquarius joins with Aquarius to form a double air element, giving rise to the kind of turbulence found in a gale-force wind!

When you enter a relationship together, a world-shattering uprising is likely to occur. Your lives are destined to produce a very unique set of circumstances and you'll be setting yourself apart from your peer group. When you walk into a room, people will feel your electrical energy and sense your individuality.

Upside? Well, you both have incredible minds and a fascination for what makes the other tick. This genuine interest in each other will propel the relationship forward. If you sense that this love affair is a tough one, you'll both do your best to try to make it work, even if it seems 'the writing is on the wall'. Neither of you gives up that easily, which is one of the predominant traits of the fixed signs—determination. In your life together, all I can say is that you should expect the unexpected.

A reasonably stable relationship is likely if you team up with an Aquarian born between the 21st and the 30th of January. These characters seem to be the best match for other Aquarians.

Aquarians born between the 31st of January and the 8th of February are not particularly well suited to each other. There's an additional influence of Virgo in people born during this time frame, which can create considerable instability and some harsh criticism on their part. This may not be a long-lasting relationship, so tread warily.

You can feel comfortable in the presence of Aquarians born between the 9th and the 19th of February due to the additional influence of Venus. They will easily express their love and warmth to you, and could even be quite tactile. This also makes for a great friendship and camaraderie.

AQUARIUS + PISCES

Air + Water = Rain

If you thought the Aquarius–Aquarius combination was complex, get ready for this one: Aquarius and Pisces! This relationship and the karmic influences between you relate strongly to your sexual expression together. Both of you will be aware of this in your first meeting.

It will be an extraordinary, unusual relationship. Sometimes, when an Aquarian and Piscean join together, there's a social or cultural taboo involved, which means you are not able to share your love honestly with others, especially your families. Sometimes the religious or cultural viewpoints of your peer groups are opposed to the relationship. There's also a hint of the clandestine when Aquarius and Pisces associate with each other. Yours could be a secretive affair.

In the extreme, Aquarius and Pisces could be said to have an impersonal connection to each other, which is why talking about your emotions and personal love seems almost a contradiction, possibly even irrelevant.

Karma and the forces of nature will bring the two of you together, and will also play havoc with your lives. Both of you will need to surrender to the storm of destiny likely to descend upon you.

Firstly, I advise you to drop your intellectual clap-trap with your Pisces partner. Pisces is a feeler and intuits life from another place to you. If you want their trust you need to get in tune with their hearts. The mind stuff can come later. Build the bridge between your Aquarian heart and their Piscean soul.

Pisces is selfless, spiritual and highly evolved. (Sorry to say it, but yes, even a little more evolved than you, Aquarius!) So try to learn the mystical lesson of life from them and know that deeper love will spring forth from your heart in due course.

Once you've proved your love is genuine, Pisces will not disappoint you, even if they appear to be 'off with the fairies' at times. There is hope for this match, but you must dive into the Piscean slip-stream of life to appreciate it to the fullest. Theirs is a magical love with which you will be blessed.

Pisces born between the 20th and the 28th or 29th of February are likely to draw you into a secretive type of relationship and it may be loaded with tension. There are some karmic lessons that both of you will have to learn through your association.

Generally Pisceans are quite sensitive, but those born between the 1st and the 10th of March are more so. Thus you need to be particularly on guard when dealing with them so as to not damage their emotions. Tread lightly and you'll be richly rewarded by your experiences with them.

Pisces born between the 11th and the 20th of March will work well with you, so there's a strong commercial and professional link between the two of you.

AQUARIUS

2010: The Year Ahead

Never take life seriously. Nobody gets out alive, anyways.

—Anonymous

Romance and friendship

The year 2010 is certainly a challenging one for you, but it will be most exciting as well! As an Aquarian you have a revolutionary personality and love the thrill of the unexpected. With the world going through such turmoil everywhere, you feel up to the task of breaking through any barriers and putting together the pieces of a rather complicated jigsaw in the coming twelve months.

Your romantic life should be bigger and brighter than it has been for many years. In January, when Neptune helps Mars and Jupiter to activate this important personal part of your horoscope, you'll be making extra efforts to enjoy this aspect of your life.

Mars and Jupiter are well known for their excessive influence on the world, and that's exactly what you can expect in the first part of the year. So please be warned: you're likely to overdo things, push yourself beyond your limits and also expect more from others than they can reasonably give to you. This could cause some frustrations and possibly even some unexpected outbursts due to the combative nature of Mars. I would hope that the Sun and Venus, which are at the same time in the quiet zone of your horoscope, will help tone down your rather reactive temperament.

In February when the Sun returns to its birth position of Aquarius, you will feel activated, energised and really confident about yourself. This is always a good omen, for it can help you extend your circle of influence and attract many new people into your life. You're idealistic this month as well, so be careful not to be taken for a ride when you meet people who are just too good to be true. This could happen as a result of the love planet Venus coming into contact with Neptune around the 8th.

You are creative and have many new ideas that you wish to share with others. This is a time when you can rally together some peer support for your concepts and use your social interactions to vent your creative expressions. There is a lot of luck in the air, so don't be surprised to meet someone who sweeps you off your feet. You may also be the recipient of flattery, good news or even gifts. But don't get carried away because sometimes there are ulterior motives behind why others do things and your ego may get the better of you. Someone could be using you to gain leverage or an advantage through the people you know, and what you can do for them.

March is an exciting time again when Venus connects with your ruling planet Uranus, bringing with it exciting and electric love affairs. If you've been in a dull relationship, feeling as if you're not getting anywhere, things can change dramatically during this particular cycle.

You're likely to do things at the drop of a hat, be attracted to the idea of spontaneous love, but you may also be harangued by doubts about the one you love. This is a time when you need to speak about your feelings and some of the deeper needs you might have that haven't yet been completely fulfilled. And another thing, don't expect everyone else to be supplying you with these needs. You have to take full responsibility for making yourself happy and not expect others to fulfil your unresolved desires.

The new Moon takes place in your zone of communications during April. It is actually an excellent time to speak about how you feel and intensify the intimacy of your personal relationships. Those of you who are married or in long-term committed relationships in particular, can expect an improvement in your affairs. If you've been scared to speak about something on your mind or within your heart because your partner hasn't been receptive or open enough, seize the moment. It's time for you to change the balance of power and reclaim your position in the relationship.

Your domestic affairs climb to the top of your agenda throughout the month of April as well when Venus brings with it love, creativity and closeness with not just your immediate family but your historic family as well. Relationships should go smoothly and if there have been some problems with the odd relative here or there, you can look forward to these relationships being much smoother from here on in.

In May, your charm will bring you many social opportunities. The Sun is high up in your chart and has a wonderful collection with Venus, especially in the first week of the month. Use this to your advantage and don't be afraid to ask for what you want. It's hardly likely that anyone will refuse you, even if you think you're expecting a little too much of them. That's the power of Venus!

As you hit the halfway mark in 2010 you may have some problems with relationships because Neptune and Mars will make you confused and unable to materialise some of your deeper desires. Others will be cagey and could try to hoodwink you in some way. Be wary of gossip and don't try to be too evasive when people ask you questions. Even if you risk hurting their feelings, it's best to be transparent and speak what's on your mind. You may lose a friend or two during this period, but at least you can say you 'called a spade a spade'.

You will be feeling quite a bit of tension in balancing the old with the new, but this has always been part of the Aquarian dilemma, hasn't it? With Saturn and Uranus challenging each other towards the end of July, this problem could reach unmanageable proportions and you will be forced to do something about it. You will not let anyone oppose your changes of mind. If they find it hard to keep up with your desire to transform your life and your relationships, they may be left behind in this whole new 'lifestyle renovation', if I can call it that. This won't bother you because you will feel a sense of urgency for cleaning out your emotional cupboards, so to speak.

If it wasn't for the beneficial hand of Jupiter in August this might be a terrible month for your love affairs, but things should work out in the end. I say this because Mars and Saturn combine to create quite a bit of negative energy, especially when it comes to your belief systems. This is the type of cycle that makes it hard for you to feel comfortable with others, particularly when the differences in your philosophy and outlook become very noticeable.

It's best to find similarities rather than differences, otherwise you'll end up becoming very frustrated. Children may also be a source of contention at this time and you need to remember who is the adult and who is the child. Aquarian parents, take note! It could be you've slackened your discipline with the youngsters and now, as they say, 'the tail is wagging the dog'. If you're feeling exasperated by this situation, you've got no one to blame but yourself, you know that.

Your energy levels peak in September with Mars dominating the celestial landscape. However, you need to harness this energy because you are likely to be a little heavy-handed with those around you. Your passion could be quite strong when Mars and Venus combine to make you much more amorous than usual. There's no point feeling guilty about this, and I hope you have someone to share these loving energies with.

Incidentally, with such a strong collection of

planetary energy in your zone of travels, I'd be surprised if you weren't planning to go somewhere to get away from the hustle and bustle of your normal day-to-day life. This is an excellent time for a second honeymoon, a rendezvous with someone you've met from afar, or just simply getting away from it all to nurture your inner self.

In the last couple of months of the year both the Sun and Mars bring with them an uplifting influence to your social life and the opportunity to connect with friends on a deeper and more meaningful level. You feel you want friends who are pro-active, not just sitting there in the background wearing a label saying 'I am a friend'.

Some of your everyday peers will wonder what's come over you when you make some additional demands on them to prove their worthiness. Please realise there are ways and means of doing this without being overbearing. It is possible test people without appearing to test them.

This quest will continue to be a theme throughout 2010 as you seek a change of style in your approach to people. Particularly towards the end of November, you may clear up some misunderstandings and gain a tremendous amount of encouragement as a result. Let me say this: you are at least able to sort out those who are true and those who are fake.

Your ruling planet Uranus moves forward on the 6th of December and this is an excellent omen for a positive march into the coming year. You will have learned a lot about your friendships, relationships and most intimate personal connections. The lunar eclipse on the 22nd is a wonderful planetary event occurring in your zone of love affairs. This further adds fuel to the fire of love and indicates that this is a time of change and positive upliftment for your love life.

Work and money

Usually people are either lucky or they have to work hard when it comes to gaining success through their professional activities. In your case, Aquarius, it appears you'll need a bit of both to propel you forward in your career and working life in 2010.

I say you'll work hard because Mars, the planet of industry and drive, influences your Sun sign from the proud and dynamic sign of Leo. This gives you the energy and ability to crush your enemies and work long and hard to achieve your goals through the coming twelve months.

In the case of Jupiter, you have some tremendous luck behind you, but don't waste it because this planet will move out of your Sun sign in the latter part of January. 'Make hay while the Sun shines!' Use this combination of planetary energies to set up the foundation for a productive year and don't waste the benefits now at your disposal.

When Jupiter moves to your zone of finances after the 18th, you will find ample opportunities to increase your income and stabilise your finances. 'The world is in terrible turmoil; finances are tight and it's hard to get work' may be the reactive thoughts emerging from your mind as I say this, but remove these negative vibrations from your being because you have a grand chance to rise above all sorts of limitations throughout 2010. You simply have to believe that you can do it, and it will happen.

Money could burn a hole in your pocket in February and also March when overconfidence could spill into the way you manage your finances. Maintain a cautious attitude. Yes, you may be lucky, but you must still exercise caution and not be wasteful.

Try to be reconciliatory in your relationships, especially when it comes to business negotiations throughout March and April. Around this time you may have to make some concessions to the demands of others, particularly if you run an independent business. You'll come to realise you can't always have your own way. However, in the end you might be pleased to note that something you initially thought was against your best interests is actually a blessing in disguise.

From the 1st of April Jupiter casts a beneficial glance on your career sector and at this time a wonderful professional opportunity may be presented to you. Your resolve, excellent work skills and persuasive communications will give you the opportunity you've been waiting for. Some of the more timid star signs of the zodiac would shy away from taking daring action, but fortunately the

Aquarian temperament is not averse to change and the unknown. You must be diplomatic in moving from one position to another, particularly if you've been in the same role for sometime and others have been relying upon you. Don't say anything until you're 100 per cent certain you want to make the big break.

There may be challenges from superiors in May due to the difficult and complex patterns of energy from the Sun and Mars. You must utilise the steadying influence of Saturn after the middle of the month to prove you are responsible and not simply shooting from the hip. You will gain the respect of employers by controlling yourself during this phase of the year.

You need to have serious discussions about loans, debts and other financial issues that involve others. You may want to make some important decisions on your own, but if you do this you could incur a backlash from those who feel you should have informed them of your actions beforehand. This will be particularly relevant if you share a business partnership. It's not a bad time to put your money into less speculative ventures and remove debt from your life while Mars and Saturn occupy your zone of shared resources. This should be the case up until September.

Legal work or documentation that requires intense focus and other bureaucratic obstructions could make life difficult for you throughout September and October. In fact, you may need to rely on the assistance of someone who has a more specialised form of knowledge and better connections than yourself to help get you through some complicated professional tangles. If you are offered help, take it and don't pretend to know more than you do. Otherwise you will only make things worse.

Mars, Venus and Mercury all offer assistance to you in the closing months of the year. In particular, November and December are lucky and satisfying because Venus softens the energy surrounding your working life. When I mention such things as career, however, this also includes people who are homemakers and work behind the scenes in a sheltered environment. In short, you should enjoy whatever you do, which in turn will attract the attention of those who count. You may be singled out for your good deeds and expertise and should therefore feel happy when I say that 2010 will finish on a rather positive note for your professional activities.

Karma, luck and meditation

I've already mentioned just how lucky you can be at the outset of 2010 due to the presence of Jupiter in your Sun sign. It's important you don't waste any opportunities likely to arise. In the latter part of January, Jupiter's influence could lessen to some extent and that's why you need to capitalise on it and focus its energy early so you don't regret not using its power.

Utilise your awareness and spiritual insights this year because Jupiter will continue to bless you, particularly financially, when it moves into your zone of money throughout January but more significantly after the 18th. There may be a sudden influx of money or some new opportunities in your work when this happens. Also, family affairs can start to improve at this time. For women who have married and happened to be born under the sign of Aquarius, the birth of children may also be on the cards.

A new phase of personal happiness, peace and prosperity, particularly in your family, is likely to occur after the new Moon of the 14th of May. This occurs in your zone of domestic happiness. Not many astrologers are aware of it but this event also relates to one's sense of fulfilment. If you are able to cultivate this sense of peace and satisfaction, it will have a marked impact on the world around you, influencing every area of your life. This time will certainly be one of the luckier transition points of the year.

As far as romance and love affairs are concerned, your karma is lucky for you in the months of May, July, and August and once again in November. The planets at this time bring with them a dose of positive love and intimacy and will inject your life with wonderful vibrations. During these periods you will attract those who not only satisfy you emotionally but who are in a position to 'show you the way' spiritually, physically and financially.

AQUARIUS

2010: Month by Month Predictions

JANUARY

The purpose of life is to fight maturity.

—Dick Werthimer

Highlights of the month

You need to clear out some of the dead wood in your life this month, particularly before Jupiter moves into your finance zone. Between the 1st and the 12th you'll be busy due to the lunar eclipse in your zone of private affairs, prompting you to remove anything that may be obstructing your relationships and other personal affairs.

Holding onto grudges can cause an explosion after the 12th because Mars will be irritating you and Saturn will be building up a high level of frustration in you until after the 18th. You need to react less strongly to what others say to you.

Finances are set to make great headway after the middle of the month and, with Venus receiving the steadying influence of Saturn around the 22nd, you'll be less likely to go on any spending sprees, which are also probably part of the reason why you're feeling a little down and out.

Mars and the Sun lift your optimism, but perhaps a little too much around the 24th, when your vitality rises and you'll be ready, raring and primed for action. This is a great physical period and one that should spur you on to take up a new gym membership and generally get out and about and mobile. This will be a great time to improve your health.

As well as utilising these physically positive energies for your health and vitality, you can enjoy a high level of confidence in your work and your financial transactions, which has to do with the responsible combination of the Sun and Saturn on the 25th of January. A coveted role or new position in your workplace is a distinct possibility at this time. But take note: you'll have to work hard and shoulder some additional burdens if you are to accept the challenge.

From the 27th till the 30th, Venus and Mars stimulate your passions. You will want to indulge your social and sexual appetites and will more than likely have ample opportunity in which to express your primal feelings.

January is an excellent time to get close to the ones you love; however, as the old saying goes, 'familiarity breeds contempt', so this is a double-edged sword. Remember to give the one you love enough space to explore his or her own creativity and request that they reciprocate by giving you ample space as well.

Venus transits into your Sun sign on the 31st. This is a wonderful cycle that makes you feel more attractive and conscious of how others perceive you. You mustn't feel guilty about pampering yourself, giving yourself a facial, a beauty session or massage. These are important elements of life that can also make you feel good and create further opportunity for you.

The last few days of January should be socially exciting with some new friend entering your life.

Romance and friendship

New problems require new responses on the 2nd when the Moon enters your zone of relationships. It will be easy to overreact to the statements of your spouse or lover, so try a new response and one that utilises more self-control. This approach should do the trick.

On the 4th, 5th and 6th your passions will be particularly fired up and you'll be receptive to the advances of your lover. You need to get plenty of rest, however, because you'll be burning the candle at both ends!

Between the 7th and 10th you may be feeling a little down and out of sorts. This mood will pass, but it's best not to spend the time with other people.

On the 11th, you're much more energised and unresolved issues with friends may finally come to a conclusion around the 12th when both sides are prepared to bury the hatchet.

Saturn moves into its retrograde movement around the 13th, indicating a desire to clear out some memories from your past. If something you've said or done has left an indelible mark on your heart, this is the time to purge yourself and move forward with a fresh slate.

You may feel quite open and friendly on the exterior but rather tense beneath the surface between the 15th and 17th. It may be necessary to hide your feelings and not reveal your intentions, which could make you feel somewhat underhanded. While no harm is intended, you mustn't allow yourself to harbour guilt.

Venus enters your zone of self-esteem around the 19th. This is an excellent time to regenerate your self-image, do something nice for yourself and tap into what's great about YOU. You will have the chance to attract new friends and opportunities in your personal life.

Unexpected opportunities are also available between the 20th and 25th when the Moon makes contact with Uranus in your zone of communications, and then on the 25th in the area of your horoscope relating to love affairs, creativity and youngsters. You can expect a great time, but once again try not to burn the midnight oil.

Wonderful discussions bring you closer to loved ones between the 29th and 31st. Extending your knowledge base is important in keeping your communications stimulating and forward thinking.

Work and money

You are more ambitious between the 3rd and 6th and you should use your time wisely. There could be some high-tech obstacles for you between the 13th and the 18th, but connecting with those who are in the know will help smooth over these problems.

You mustn't cut corners if you are trying to complete an extra amount of work this month. Set the trend for the year by getting organised and not overlooking the trivial responsibilities that will be presented to you.

Contracts are favoured after the 21st, but you may need to do much more homework than you thought initially. This may require some extra time spent away from family and friends to get it just right.

Don't let disagreements about money blow out of proportion between the 27th and 30th. If you look carefully at this situation you'll realise you yourself haven't been beyond reproach and could have been better at managing your own finances.

On the 31st, a telephone call, which is at first distracting, will end up saving you much more time than you had first expected.

Destiny dates

Positive: 1, 3, 4, 5, 6, 11, 19, 20, 21, 22, 23, 24, 25, 31

Negative: 14, 18

Mixed: 2, 7, 8, 9, 10, 12, 13, 15, 16, 17, 27, 28, 29, 30

FEBRUARY

Highlights of the month

Up to the 14th, when the new Moon occurs, you will be researching, investigating and actively seeking answers to your life's problems and challenges. This is not a bad thing, so don't take what I'm saying negatively. You'll be curious and using your mind to break through old patterns of behaviour to improve yourself and the relationships in which you're currently involved. This is all good stuff.

Your creative appetite is powerful. You are hungry to share your talents with others. When the Sun comes together with Neptune after the 15th, you will be inspired to translate your experiences into something wonderful, creative and possibly even spiritual.

There is a note of warning to be attached to this specific planetary cycle, however. A form of self-deception or confusion and doubt may also be part of the equation. You mustn't be so overwhelmed by excitement that you don't look into the credentials of others with whom you happen to be sharing your ideas. In the worst-case scenario, you may be taken advantage of and may thoroughly regret trusting someone. Don't feel bad about testing others during this phase of the year.

You are likely to experience some good fortune after the 17th when Venus comes together with Jupiter in your zone of finances. This is one of the luckiest combinations of the zodiac and also has a bearing on your family life to some extent. Good news through your social networks and relatives can be expected. Gifts are also not out of the question, either in terms of receiving them or giving them.

Try to curb your confidence in financial matters this month, especially towards the end of the month when the Sun attempts to burn a hole in your pocket around the 19th. You may feel as though you have money to burn, when in fact, if you scrutinise your monetary affairs more closely, you'll realise you have extended yourself a little too much.

You're all fired up again when Venus casts its trine aspect on your career sector between the 25th and the 28th. Once again, some lucky celestial energy is likely to put you in the right place just at the right time and this offers you an opportunity to further your professional ambitions. Someone you meet in a social circumstance will be instrumental in helping to open a few doors for you.

When the Sun makes its move through your zone of finances, it also influences your speech and your power of persuasion. You'll be able to convince others of what you want and they're likely to agree without too much obstruction.

Romance and friendship

Venus continues to be in full swing this month, offering you a better state of mind, a passionate outlook and a sense of excitement about your life generally. From the 1st to the 5th you will be shining and others will see it. However, don't use this to your advantage if you have to step on another's toes to fulfil your desires.

Between the 5th and 8th there could be some irritating discussions that go around in circles. If you can't convince a friend of your position, what's the point of continuing the dialogue? On the 9th and 10th it's not a bad idea to pick apart your dreams to gain an insight into your relationships through a spiritual 'backdoor', so to speak.

You may also have itchy feet and will want to travel, if only for a day or two. This could mean getting away from everyone to be alone. It will recharge your emotional, mental and spiritual batteries.

Family affairs between the 14th and 15th are happy but could run into confusion when you are asked to help someone make a rather difficult decision. Listen carefully without committing yourself either way, because you won't want to feel guilty later about leading them up the garden path.

You feel the need to change your lifestyle between the 17th and 19th, so if you're looking at new diets or weight loss, try to avoid short-lived fads. Bear in mind that much of this mood has to do with your mental state, not just how you look.

You can feel confident about the future of your romance after the 22nd. Venus, the Sun and Neptune all support your vision for what you believe you deserve romantically. What's more, your partner may be more amenable to making gestures of love and demonstrating just how he or she feels about you. This will further encourage you to make greater efforts yourself.

At the close of the month when the Moon again contacts Mars you may want to plan a sexy night out on the town with your lover. On the 28th when the Moon activates your deeper passionate and sexual nature as well, you may find yourself talking about deep and meaningful topics simply because you've been able to let down your guard and your partner has also removed their so-called 'mask'. This is a period of deepening your attachment to the ones you love.

Work and money

You can't always use your charm and persuasiveness to overcome procedural complications in the workplace. Between the 3rd and 5th, pay special attention to the way things are done rather than the way they should be done. If others are interfering, you could run into strife around the 6th. Stick to your guns because you are probably correct about what needs to be done and by when.

Although you have an opportunity to earn some extra cash on the 7th, you may blow it all by the 9th feeling that retail therapy is the way out. This will only create more burdens for you over the coming days.

You could increase your level of communication and things should get busy for you leading up to the 17th. After this time a short business trip, which could also be fun, may be necessary.

On or about the 18th to the 23rd you are lucky and could win something, perhaps a bonus or a better position within your current business.

You feel talented but mustn't brag about your achievements after the 26th because someone in close quarters may start to exhibit jealousy.

Destiny dates

Positive: 1, 2, 9, 10, 14, 15, 17, 18, 20, 21, 22, 23, 25, 27, 28

Negative: 6, 8

Mixed: 3, 4, 5, 7, 19, 26

MARCH

Highlights of the month

It's more than likely you will have to give some careful thought as to how you are going to restructure the commercial side of your business, the budgetary expenses of your family, and your value system generally this month. Furthermore, Venus enters this very zone of finance and conjoins the electric and unpredictable planet that rules Aquarius, Uranus, on the 4th.

There could be a roller-coaster ride in store for many Aquarians who haven't done their homework on such things as tax, superannuation and other savings and budgetary measures. If you're one of those people, might I suggest you 'grab the bull by the horns' and do it now! It's never too late to steer yourself in a better direction, even if some of those changes are a little unpleasant.

Venus quickly exits your zone of finance on the 7th to bring you powerful communications, interesting conversations and also a new phase of learning.

This will stimulate your mental and cultural interests, so expect yourself to be surrounded by people who inspire you to learn more and expand your personal horizons.

This is a time when journeys will be pleasant, when connections with your relatives, siblings and your neighbours will also be rather light and breezy. If you haven't had much to do with your next-door neighbour or your local community, this could well be a time when you're invited to open your heart and learn a little bit about them in the same way that they want to learn about you. Community projects could captivate the attention of some Aquarians during this Venus cycle. Take some time out to arrange a seductive night with your partner or lover after the 8th.

You mustn't let the tough opposition of Venus and Saturn deter you from making friends and getting out on the town after the 9th. You may have a tendency to want to stay to yourself, but it's best for you to make an extra effort.

The period of the 17th till the 22nd is important in that your wilful, independent nature may be at odds with others in your environment. Try not to be too pushy in forcing your ideas down other people's throats. If you're respectful and gently persuasive in the way you offer your concepts, the responses will be far more favourable and productive.

Romance and friendship

Connections with older males, perhaps a parental figure or older sibling, will require quite a bit of your energy between the 2nd and the 6th. If traditionally this person has been domineering in your life, you'll now be able to take full control of your destiny and let them know this fact.

The social scene heats up for you after the 7th, with plenty of invitations to join in with unusual and exciting people. But be careful around the 9th when your emotions could become very intense and your demands for people to prove their love to you might set them offside.

You are very emotional between the 13th and 15th and may say or do something you later regret. Think twice before opening your mouth and possibly embarrassing yourself in front of others.

From the 19th till the 24th you might start to feel you are out of step with your loved one, particularly if you are in a long-term relationship or marriage. Your energy could start to wane a little while theirs starts to wax, making you feel as if you are travelling in different directions emotionally.

The problem with many people is that they feel the highs and lows of their personal lives must always be in sync, and this just can't happen! Accept that this is a time where you both need to spend some time away from each other, gather your energies and come back with a revitalised attitude.

After the 25th your doubts could cause you to do some rash and rather unexpected things. A desire for excitement, a novel investigation, might cause you to stumble upon someone who is very different from yourself. You may want to develop a new relationship at this time but will also fear the unknown. You may have no choice but to transcend your past concepts about what attracts you and try something new. This is a time where relationships may also be discarded in favour of something fresh and vital.

Work and money

You have a tremendous intellectual curiosity this month and in particular from the 3rd you'll be ferreting out new titbits of information on how you can earn money, how to invest it and what sorts of activities will give you the best shot at ensuring a bright and successful financial future.

Several planets in your finance sector show there is an accent on earnings and investigating your bank accounts, taxation and other financial investments or debts.

Things should go smoothly up to the 8th, after which time an error in your bookkeeping may cause you a little fright. This glitch will be easily rectified and may not be quite as bad as you first thought.

You are emotional about your spending habits after the 15th, so try to think twice before purchasing that much-desired item, especially if it's not absolutely necessary.

You may be able to extend your newfound knowledge to help a friend who may be in financial dire straits after the 25th. You'll need to go easy on them because it will be glaringly obvious they have overspent or simply been wasteful in the way they have used their money.

Destiny dates

Positive: 2, 3, 4, 5, 6, 7, 8

Negative: 13, 14, 15, 17, 18

Mixed: 9, 19, 20, 21, 22, 23, 24, 25

APRIL

Highlights of the month

Saturn places a little more pressure on you this month as it returns to revisit your zone of joint finances and monetary issues. It could be that because Venus is stimulating your desire for luxury in the home area, your expenses might increase between the 1st and the 8th. I'd suggest you discuss your financial plans before entering into any agreements. Otherwise you might experience a backlash from your spouse or partner.

You have quite a bit of imagination to overcome any emotional or professional tangles, due to the Moon activating your zone of career. Although you may have pressure on several fronts you'll take pleasure in working out a systematic plan to overcome these difficulties. Women may also be an important influence in your professional sphere.

Your knowledge base increases from April, with Jupiter casting a favourable glance on your professional activities. You can learn to do something you've done for a long while in a different way so that it will ultimately save you a lot of time. These new methodologies will also eventually help you reap the rewards by way of new financial opportunities, cash bonuses or other unexpected increases in income.

The combination of Mercury and Venus is an excellent pattern of energy for most Aquarians during this month, which means you'll be interested in creative pursuits, high-level communications and anything that can culturally expand your horizons. However, you may find that, after the 15th, you're a little less inclined to think and will be more interested in socialising with friends and getting out and about rather than taking too many responsibilities on board.

You must again seriously reappraise your budget, with Venus and Saturn entering into a fine relationship around the 24th. Don't let money get in the road of good relationships. Or rather, I should say, don't sweep these issues under the rug. They will in turn create havoc for you. Open, transparent communication, especially if you feel uncomfortable about the way your partner or a friend is dealing with your money, means you must speak up, and do so now.

Romantic pursuits are very much favoured when Venus enters your zone of love affairs on the 25th. You may feel your heart missing a beat if you happen to come across a new person or are introduced to an individual who shows some interest in you. Of course, if you're currently attached, this may be a little uncomfortable. But why not use this energy to stimulate your existing relationship by doing something a little out of the ordinary?

If you're thinking of turning over a new leaf, you can do so after the 26th, when the Sun triangulates Pluto. This is your chance to overcome some of your weaknesses, lingering habits, and to become a much better person. If you're smoking, drinking too much or generally not feeling on top of things, this will be an excellent time to make a commitment to yourself.

Romance and friendship

Between the 1st and the 5th you may have a strong desire to spend time at home with your family but will not be able to give in to these sentimental urges due to other more pressing demands.

Up to the 7th you will be able to reach out to someone who's been rather distant or appears angry with you for some reason. You may have misinterpreted their intentions and this is a time of healing.

The new Moon for this month takes place on the 14th in your zone of communications and is an excellent omen that brings you into contact with people near and far. If you've not yet developed your taste for Internet communication, this could be a month in which you open the door to a whole new vista of social and romantic opportunities. Your home life is your main focus between the 16th and the 19th. A new romance emerges around the 17th.

Trifling health matters are a bother between the 19th and 22nd, but don't disregard your body's inner signals. You may feel that something this trivial may not be necessary to take time off for; however, it's best not to postpone health matters this month.

Venus enters your fifth zone of love affairs on the 25th. This is one of the best cycles for love and romance and any rendezvous you plan now is likely to be a smashing success. You are feeling emotionally elated and ready to meet your soulmate.

The month finishes on a good note with a lovely, exciting meeting with friends or a lover in a rather unusual setting between the 26 and 30th.

Work and money

You want to loosen up and enjoy your money, but Saturn will cause you to become extremely heavy and serious about these issues throughout April, especially between the 5th and 8th.

It's important you reconcile yourself to the idea that work is predominantly about the passion, love and skill you have in executing your duties rather than actually what you gain from the chore. Reconnect with these deeper principles and the meaning of work will make you feel much happier, even if you don't have as much money as you'd like.

Sometime after the 12th you might not find it all that easy to keep up with peer group pressure, fashion and other expensive activities that require splurging on your part. For the sake of keeping up with the Jones's, you may outwardly feign conformity only to regret secretly the fact that you are spending so much money on useless things and activities. As much as being a time that requires a reappraisal of the way you use and value money, it is probably more a case of re-evaluating your friends and their philosophies as well.

After the 25th and up until the 28th you might have some successes in the speculative markets such as the stock market and other riskier ventures.

Destiny dates

Positive: 14, 15, 16, 17, 18, 25, 26, 27, 28, 29, 30

Negative: 8, 12, 20, 21, 22, 24

Mixed: 1, 2, 3, 4, 5, 6, 7, 19

MAY

Highlights of the month

Venus continues to trek through your zone of creativity and romance throughout the month of May but, between the 1st and the 3rd, you might feel a little sentimental and this could impact upon one or another of your friendships. Try to speak clearly from the head, rather than letting your emotions get the better of you.

Develop hobbies and pastimes that engage your creative self along with social interests between the 1st and the 5th. You are charming at this time and also able to express freely some of your deeper feelings in a creative way. Painting, music, dance and live theatre would be excellent ways to spend your time in the first week of the month.

You could be at odds with your employer between the 8th and the 10th, with the Sun moving well away from your career zone. You might simply have had enough and need a little space away from the day-to-day grind of work. If there's pressure, you will succumb and find yourself regretting the decision to give in. Only you know whether or not you're prepared to yield to pressure rather than follow your own heart. Be wary of accidents, injuries, mishaps or other misunderstandings between the 10th and the 15th. Mars will spur you on to do things that are rather impulsive and risky.

Something of a milestone can be reached by the 19th when Venus and Neptune, the idealistic planet, produce favourable vibrations in your life. You might meet your soulmate or come to understand the true meaning of your current relationship. You may not be able to articulate easily what you are feeling but there is no doubt that you will feel something very special about these energies.

It's very important to feel comfortable about your work space, and when Venus enters your zone of work and daily activities on the 20th, you'll be more conscious of how clutter and untidiness is affecting your mind and your performance. You may have to take some time out to do a mini spring-cleaning to create a more favourable environment in which to conduct your business and creative affairs.

Developing a greater consistency in your pattern of saving and management of money will be evident after the 23rd. With Jupiter and Saturn playing seesaw—one planet, Jupiter, indicating expansion and the other, Saturn, referring to contraction—it shows just how inconsistent you may be in these matters. Finding the happy balance will of course be a task that you will take rather seriously.

Don't allow others to manipulate you between the 24th and the 28th. You'll know who I'm talking about: it's essential for you to play the power game as cleverly and shrewdly as possible. This is an opportunity for you to understand the psychology of love and the mechanics of how people try to usurp others and gain the upper hand. Don't make decisions quickly because this will only give others a chance to control you.

Romance and friendship

Your heart could be torn between two people between the 1st and 3rd. This is particularly aimed more at Aquarians who are single, but on occasion may also affect you if you are married, too, so be careful!

You definitely have a charming aura about you and will be likely to attract more than one potential soulmate during this cycle.

The 6th till the 10th is also promising in respect of your love life and your generous actions will not go unnoticed by others. There is a philanthropic side of your personality coming through now and you will want to help others simply for the sake of doing a good turn.

A family pow-wow will be high on your agenda of things to do when the Moon transits your zone of domestic activities around the 12th. Make your feelings known up to the 14th and, if your family schedule or the house itself needs work, it's a great time to enlist the joint support of all family members to get the job done!

You could feel youthful again between the 16th and 19th when you find yourself surrounded by a cluster of young people with fresh new ideas. You are likely to realise they are not so far-fetched, after all. You might come under fire for thinking a little differently to the accepted norm, particularly by peers who are your age or a little older, but don't let this deter you from enjoying life and finding out what works for you.

There's nothing like an adversary to rekindle your feelings for the one you love and between the 17th and 22nd it's likely you might suspect your partner is flirting just a little too much, or maybe more! This will quickly mobilise your emotional resources to pull them back into line, which may interestingly work to cement your bond of love and take your relationship to the next level. If your partner travels frequently and has been conspicuously absent emotionally, you must remember the old saying that 'absence makes the heart grow fonder, but too much absence makes it wander'.

On the 31st your dreams and aspirations move into high gear as Neptune moves retrograde. You can use creative visualisation to start making things happen in your life, especially if you feel as though life has been slow in coming forward in offering you what you think you deserve.

Work and money

Mars continues to spend much of its time in your zone of partnerships and public relations this year, so it should come as no surprise to you that even throughout May you will be very focused on making headway in this area of your life.

Between the 5th and the 10th, put aside time to catch up with old business associates, clients and even work colleagues who have in the past helped you achieve your goals. Remember to show your gratitude, even if there's nothing to be gained immediately financially or commercially through the contact. These gestures of goodwill will hold you in good stead and turn things around for you, bringing you greater success in the coming months.

There are diametrically opposing forces influencing your financial zone throughout May. With Saturn and Jupiter in conflict and Uranus also playing its part, any decisions you make surrounding money may hang delicately in the balance, so seek the advice of a third party if you are not sure what to do. The decision could have intense ramifications for the future.

Malicious gossip is not something in which you want to embroil yourself after the 17th, when rumours on the grapevine could damage you and others in the process. It will be tempting to get involved and put in your twenty cents' worth, but my suggestion is that you leave it well alone. And besides, if you have time to talk about the trivial affairs of others, it shows you are probably not focusing enough on your own work.

You have some challenging but exciting events happening in the workplace between the 25th and

29th. This could be a time when your confidence is reinstated, with some good news for a possible promotion or pay rise.

Destiny dates

Positive: 7, 16, 18, 19, 20, 21, 22, 29, 31

Negative: 24

Mixed: 1, 2, 3, 4, 5, 6, 8, 9, 10, 11, 12, 13, 14, 17, 23, 25, 26, 27, 28

JUNE

Highlights of the month

The new Moon occurs in your fifth zone of love affairs this month and therefore you can expect some revitalisation of your personal matters, particularly those regarding love and sex. For Aquarians who are single, you might find yourself enamoured by another person and have the universe's full blessing to explore this and enjoy it to the max.

You have a dose of self-confidence around the 3rd, which means you won't be taking a back seat in any of your affairs, whether it is family, social or professional. You can act in the capacity of a leader this month, showing others the way. I guess the key word for you at this time of your life would be 'authority'.

Venus continues to bring you ample opportunity in your professional sphere, but Mars and Neptune have the tendency to undermine your ability to make things happen as quickly as you'd like them to. Particularly between the 5th and the 7th, you may feel paralysed to move in the direction that you wish, and may have to play the waiting game.

Things move forward a little more swiftly when the Sun provides you a window of opportunity after the 7th. Luck can come knocking at your door around the 8th and you should move quickly in case you lose an opportunity. These may be scary times because you could be feeling rather comfortable in the situation you're in, but in such an era of change, you may need to 'go with the flow' to see where the forces of life take you.

Marriage, engagements and other festivities associated with either your own or your family and friends' circumstances are very prominent between the 14th and the 20th. Venus enters your seventh zone of love and marriage, as well as creating favourable aspects to Uranus and Jupiter, which prove to be a blessing. Your life will be anything but uninteresting or dull during this phase of the year. You'll be active, on the go, and certainly very, very busy. But try to keep a hold on how things are being organised, otherwise you could find yourself being run ragged by others who are dictating your life.

Watch your health and diet after the 21st. When you're just so busy, it's easy to overlook the necessity to cook and eat in a wholesome and harmonious environment. You need to chew slowly and also surround yourself with the right sort of energies to make the experience of food a beneficial one.

You may have to contend with an adversary between the 23rd and the 26th. This may surprise you when you find out who it is. Remember that sometimes wolves do make their presence felt in sheep's clothing. Be extra alert.

A lunar eclipse on the 26th influences you for the rest of the month, and brings with it a dose of spiritual insight.

Romance and friendship

Between the 1st and 6th, relationships may not prosper as well as they should; but not because of any emotional constraints. Someone you love or a close friend may be unwell and you will not be able to exchange those warm and caring feelings as easily as usual. However, your desire to help them and selflessly put aside some time to support their needs will bring greater co-operation between you over the coming weeks.

Between the 7th and the 11th your motives may be questioned by someone and this could make you feel somewhat disappointed. You can only try your best to remain transparent and operate from a space of good intentions. After all, what others feel is completely out of your control.

Relationships begin to flourish after the 12th and you'll be feeling much more sensitive to the needs of your partner. Also, you'll feel as though they are 'on the same page' as you and not as judgemental as usual. You'll feel lucky and grateful to have the friends and relatives that you do at this time.

A difficult relationship from the past may need

to be confronted between the 14th and the 18th and, particularly with Mars and Saturn conjoining in your eighth zone of secrets, passion and other transformative energies, you need to use these influences in a positive way. Being invited to a party or get-together in which an old flame is present may be something you instinctively want to avoid, but I recommend you attend with your head held high. Don't let fear dominate your decisions.

Misunderstandings over honesty or punctuality may be a problem for you from the 19th till the 20th. You need to clarify times and meeting places and co-ordinate your diary with the one you love. What's more, make sure that your modes of communication—for example, mobile phones and computer systems—are intact so messages don't go missing. You can avoid arguments by being more organised.

You can eliminate feelings of inadequacy, shyness and other bad habits after the 26th when the lunar eclipse brings you to a clearer state of understanding. Jupiter's presence in your zone of communication also makes it easier for you now to speak up on certain matters that previously seemed to be off-limits.

Work and money

This month you can reorganise some of your workplace circumstances, especially if they have been constraining you. It is a time for breaking free from such situations and people who are limiting you in your professional life.

Between the 2nd and 5th, try not to let a sense of indebtedness determine the decisions you make. Someone may 'have you over a barrel' if they offer you assistance with a view to some sort of payback in future. It's best to do things on your own during this cycle.

Be prepared to plan if you go on a job interview because the impression you make will be lasting. Actually, have all the prerequisite paperwork available, including your résumé, past milestones and references, around the 10th. You could be so overwhelmed by this new opportunity that you'll forget or overlook some rather important aspect of the meeting.

Between the 15th and 22nd, don't turn a blind eye to sloppy work being performed on your behalf by such people as your accountant, bank manager or others in your employ. If you're paying money to these people, you should demand the best possible return for that investment. Don't be too extravagant with your money after the 19th.

Confusion surrounding an order for some goods may leave you frazzled around the 28th.

Destiny dates

Positive: 12, 26

Negative: 23, 24, 25

Mixed: 1, 2, 3, 4, 5, 6, 7, 8, 9, 10, 11, 14, 15, 16, 17, 18, 19, 20, 21, 28

JULY

Highlights of the month

Did you know that frustration is actually unresolved anger? The two principal planets involved in this emotion are Mars and Saturn. Their coming together throughout the months of July and August is telling on the way you will feel. However, by being forewarned about this you will certainly be forearmed. Take measures now to ensure you don't allow this planetary combination to influence you adversely, especially in the latter part of the month.

What are some of the things that you can do to sidestep these energies? Well, leading up to the 9th, when Venus and Neptune present you with complicated choices in your relationships, try to step back a little and not get too emotionally involved in the process. You might be aware of others dancing around you a little, trying to pull your strings and influence your way of thinking, much to your dissatisfaction. But if you are principled and stick to your guns, you'll come out of this unscathed.

There's some light relief for you between the 10th and the 23rd; firstly when Venus enters your zone of sexuality, giving you a chance to 'let off steam', if you know what I mean! This could be the time when intimacy and sexuality draws you closer to the one you love. But don't use it wholly and solely as a means of escape, because you could be defeating the purpose of dealing with problems head on. Try to use your energy in concert with other means of resolving issues throughout the month of July.

Between the 14th and the 23rd, you're interested in understanding others who have a different view on life. You are in an investigative mode, and Pluto reveals just how deep and penetrating your insights will be at this time. It's as if you have X-ray vision and can see beyond a person's words to the motives that are behind what they are saying. This is an excellent scenario if you work with people—in sales, for example, or marketing—and need to gain clear access to what makes a person 'tick'.

You could make decisions that affect the stability of your life between the 21st and the 24th. You could be bored with your usual group of friends and may opt for something a little more bizarre or out of the ordinary. This could lead you to discover new things about yourself, as well as others and the world in general. But, by the same token, it may also cause you to err. Accept the trusted advice of a friend in these matters, and don't do things that you'll later regret.

Ethical issues, legal matters and other types

of moral dilemmas could confront you around the 30th. Don't lose your cool if someone doesn't happen to understand where you're coming from on a particular point of view, especially if it happens to fall in a political or religious category. Actually, it's probably best to avoid these topics altogether.

Romance and friendship

Between the 1st and 6th, confusion surrounds much of your communications so it's best not to let excitement get in the way of dealing with these emotional troubles. And another thing: if you need to get into deep and meaningful discussions, try doing so on neutral territory for the best results.

There's a need for secrecy between the 8th and 12th and it is necessary to get to the bottom of the troubles you have had. Don't go 'airing your dirty laundry in public'.

There are powerful and positive emotions to be expected from the 13th to the 16th. In marriage and romance, feelings will be highlighted and there could be some celebrations in which you and your partner will share. It's an excellent period for your friends and for yourself as well.

Mars and Saturn cause some damage to your intimacy between the 17th and 20th. Someone is demanding more of you than you can give them. You'll have to try to find substitutes for these feelings of lack or frustration through other outlets. Unfortunately even this may not work, so you'll just have to grin and bear it.

The period between the 22nd and 24th could be a pretty tough time for you. Communication using letters and written words will be particularly valuable, especially if you are feeling tongue-tied about a particular topic. Words won't come to you easily; therefore, to gain maximum impact, put pen to paper.

From the 27th to the 30th you'll be better placed to kiss and make up with someone you love. That person may surprisingly apologise to you, so reunions are also likely in this period. By the 31st you may receive an unforeseen invitation to an exciting event or party.

Work and money

During July the combination of the Sun and Mercury will make you somewhat highly strung and overworked because your feeling is that you are not at all supported by others, especially between the 4th and 8th. You may have to stand alone to get things done.

However, discussions and significant meetings with employers between the 9th and 12th favour you, so don't be scared to ask for a little more than they are prepared to allow. Their offers will be quite genuine and generous.

Concentrate deeply on your work between the 16th and 19th. It's not a bad idea to turn off phones so that important work can get your full attention.

Jupiter moves into its retrograde motion on the 23rd, which means contracts could take an unexpected turn. New issues could arise and will need your immediate attention. Expect resolutions to be a little slower to arrive than normal.

After the 30th, legal disputes will need more investigation on your part before you state your case. Unfortunately, conclusions will elude you for a while longer.

Destiny dates

Positive: 13, 14, 15, 16, 27, 28, 29, 31

Negative: 1, 2, 3

Mixed: 4, 5, 6, 7, 8, 9, 10, 11, 12, 17, 18, 19, 20, 21, 22, 23, 24, 30

AUGUST

Highlights of the month

You mustn't assume that there's an endless supply of resources this month, and Mars and Saturn will see to it that being conservative is at the top of your list of priorities. You'll have a tendency towards extravagance, waste and misusing your resources and money as well. It would be a shame not to listen to what Mars and Saturn are saying to you in respect of feeling obstructed, for it is possibly a blessing in disguise.

It's quite okay to accept your limitations and admit you're not quite savvy enough to know exactly how to be circumspect. This is where education—that is, seeking out an understanding of the ways and means to do this—is essential throughout the month of August.

On the 4th, 5th, 7th and 9th, the energies that challenge you in these areas will be strong. You will need to have some sort of mental armoury at hand to counter the frustrating influences of Mars and Saturn. For example, if you don't have enough money to go out on the town with someone, you may feel dejected, unworthy or simply angry that life is dishing out hard times to you.

But this is precisely the type of thinking and behaviour I'm saying needs to be changed so that this period can be viewed positively. For example, this can be a month where not being able to do such things gives you the opportunity to build your nest egg and start to enjoy life to the fullest. You can begin to realise the future security you hope for can't be achieved if you simply squander all your resources and waste your money on frivolous activities.

You need the courage of your convictions after the 18th, when Mars triangulates the Sun. This comes on the heels of Uranus, the planet of unpredictability, entering your zone of finances on the 14th. This yet again means you may need to re-evaluate carefully how you're spending your money and stand firm on your decision not to yield to others' demands for you to keep up with the Jones's or to splurge.

Your passions run riot around the 21st, when Venus and Mars come together in your ninth zone of travels. If you're an enthusiastic adventurer, wanting to explore the world, then you may plan to make that happen and do it with someone whom you feel comfortable enough. And this can also be the start of a new phase of spiritual development for you. Travelling to see cultures you ordinarily wouldn't think are appealing, now somehow sparks your interest.

More esoteric forms of study are likely when the Sun enters the eighth house on the 23rd. You may be curious about how the planets, palmistry and other psychological disciplines can reveal to you the nature of your character, relationships, destiny and future. You should embark on these mental and spiritual explorations in a spirit of love, without expecting too much in return. After all—and you can take it from me—there's no quick way to learn such a vast range of subjects.

Romance and friendship

The combined influence of Mars and Saturn in your romantic life will be inhibited and your friends and lovers may feel distant, especially between the 1st and 5th. They can't or simply won't speak to you. Doesn't that make you so mad? But they may have their own problems, so don't push them too hard.

Try finding something else to occupy your attention after the 7th; something more worthwhile like a hobby or sport and connecting with a friend who understands your dilemma.

The new Moon on the 10th is a bright new omen for love and marriage. You and your partner can be confident and this will be a chance for you to kiss and make up (and make love).

Your partner or a close friend may be in a spot of financial bother between the 13th and 16th. If you are asked to help, don't push your opinions too hard; just be amenable to what they have to say and listen more than you speak. Believe it or not, this can be a great help to them.

Friends will inspire you to do your best after the 17th. A new idea will get legs around the 18th and it could be a joint pet, creative or community project that gets you all fired up. This will in turn inspire your friends to roll up their sleeves and help you achieve your goals.

A family reunion may not be your usual cup of tea but between the 24th and 27th, it will be quirkily enjoyable. Join in with an open mind and do your best to enjoy it, even if it is a little difficult at first.

Work and money

Between the 2nd and 11th you will be working on converting old or unused furniture or other clutter in your home into cash. You might have a garage sale or set up a domestic financial project that will create some surplus money for you and your family.

You could be annoyed by wasteful practices on the work scene. From the 13th to the 19th, you may have some constructive suggestions to save energy and money and will meet with welcome responses from your employer and co-workers.

Try putting some money into your education between the 21st to the 27th. This will expand your mind and horizons by travelling to investigate other cultures as well. It will be money well invested.

Destiny dates

Positive: 6, 8, 10, 11, 22, 23

Negative: 1, 19

Mixed: 2, 3, 4, 5, 9, 13, 14, 15, 16, 17, 18, 21, 24, 25, 26, 27

SEPTEMBER

Highlights of the month

You might assume that the answers to most of your life's problems are outside yourself, but this month it will be quite the opposite, Aquarius. You'll come to realise that much of what you're seeking is indeed in you, the seeker him- or herself. Maybe psychic flashes and prophetic dreams may point you in the direction you're looking for, and this is obviously something that arises from within your very own self. Between the 3rd and the 8th you can completely trust your intuition to give you the right answers to the questions you've been asking.

On the 9th, Venus brings you face to face with new goals and objectives and, if you've listened to your inner promptings, your idealism will be very well balanced with practicality. Having a deeper understanding of those for, and with, whom you work will assist you in making great headway in your professional life.

There will be many social engagements attached to the work you do. Even if you're a home-maker, you could find that social activities also seem to be strongly tied in with your day-to-day family obligations. This will be a fun period where work and play do indeed mix.

Mars is notorious for its dynamic energy and, after the 15th when it enters your work sphere, you'll be driven to reach your goals in spite of yourself. If you have planned and worked well in advance to achieve some meaningful objectives, things will go smoothly for you. The combined influence of Venus and Mars will not only make you persuasive but also very effective in executing your duties.

Your personal achievements will affect others positively. You'll be pleased to receive extra respect and admiration for what you're doing and, what's more, you'll be amused by the fact that you don't even have to make too much effort to get it. Such is the power and glory of Venus as it influences you from the highest point of your chart.

They say that nothing beats skill and competence when it comes to success, but you will have the tendency to feel a little important in the company of others around the 21st. Coupled with your confidence in what you can do, might I suggest that a little humility goes a long way, too, and will win you more friends at this time?

Don't feel too bad if you find yourself in a state of necessity around the 22nd to the 25th. However, as the old saying goes, 'necessity is the mother of invention', so many great ideas are now likely to arise when you least expect them. You'll be able to use these flashes of inspiration to streamline your work, fascinate others and persuade your employers to give you a better deal.

Romance and friendship

You mustn't let familiarity breed contempt between the 1st and 4th of September. Show your appreciation for any kindnesses offered and don't postpone that call to say thanks for some love or a gift that has been passed to you.

Venus, being high in your chart this month, is great for your personal esteem and popularity after the 9th. A measured acceptance of invitations is necessary to balance your heavy business–social agenda just now.

You'll be surrounded by friends between the 11th and 15th, so don't worry about being a wallflower. But by the same token, you must eliminate some 'dead wood' from your life: those people who don't carry their weight as friends. Someone may be using you because you can open doors for them. This is not the time to let others walk all over you and use you.

Between the 16th and 18th, shopping for gifts and taking on an organising role for a group will see you at your best and at the forefront. Do give others the tasks delegated to them so the load is shared and this way you will get more done sooner.

There are indications for the birth of children after the 23rd, which may also mean reconnecting with family and friends and reviving your own inner child. You mustn't lose touch with what makes you special and at the same time happy within. Your hunches will pay great dividends between the 28th and 30th. An insight into others is extremely valuable and a lesson learned from another's error can also help you sidestep similar mistakes.

Work and money

The combination of Venus and Mars in your work zone means 'wow': what energy and vitality! But there are always two sides to a coin, aren't there? Due to this incredible dose of energy, others may not be able or want to keep up with you between the 1st and the 10th. It may be necessary to slow down your pace and explain things a little more thoroughly to those who aren't in the same expansive mode of activity as yourself.

Your employees, those who usually assist you, may be reluctant to do so this time around. Also, I sense that 'the natives'—your subordinates—may be getting restless and ready to revolt.

Don't insulate yourself from new ideas or suggestions that can help you between the 13th and the 20th, even if you think they are a little far-fetched. If you are out of step with new trends, you'll miss the boat. Education will continue to be an important component of your life during this phase.

From the 22nd to the 24th, a short course or lecture will put you back in the commercial and professional picture of what is necessary. Try to expand your circle of understanding to include community and even global trends.

Destiny dates

Positive: 5, 6, 7, 8, 9, 10, 11, 12, 21, 22, 23, 24, 25, 28, 29, 30

Negative: none

Mixed: 1, 2, 3, 4, 13, 14, 15, 16, 17, 18, 19, 20

OCTOBER

Highlights of the month

The way in which you handle your responsibilities during October will determine the outcome of your karma for a long-time to come. You must be patient to realise the maximum effect of the efforts you put in just now. But don't jump the gun, and don't be too hard on yourself. 'All good things come to those who wait.' The Sun and Saturn are responsible for this new phase in your life and it commences between the 1st and the 4th of October.

Your love affairs and relationships could be rather embarrassingly public as Mars and Venus continue to dance their way through the upper part of your horoscope in your work sphere. If you don't want your personal affairs out in the open, it's probably best to stay away and have a quiet time at home with the one you love. Some red wine, incense and candlelight would be ideal to set the mood for you and give you the feeling that you're in control of your relationship, rather than everyone else dictating how you should act.

For single Aquarians, this could be a fun time when a secret admirer makes themselves known to you. Come on, you know that your charm is working wonders during this phase, so why would you be taken aback when you receive that telephone call or e-mail asking you out on a date?

From the 10th, any deterioration in your health is more than likely a reflection of your touchy and emotional state of being. You're probably soaking up the energy of negative people around you in your workplace, and it will be important for you to find adequate means to offload these troubles and unwanted tensions. I'll even go so far as to say that it's best to avoid those who are leaning on you for advice and sucking you dry of your positive energy.

From the 28th, you'll stand out among your peers for your unique contributions and generally easygoing way of dealing with things. This, however, may also lead to some envy from others lurking in the shadows. You must learn to keep your enemies as close to you as your friends. Don't assume everyone has your best interests at heart at this time, even though the majority of people will support you.

You'll be asked to develop more faith in your financial stability from the 21st. Even if you feel worried about how you are going to pay the next round of bills, your faith and hope are powerful driving forces to cause nature to bring you the appropriate means to deal with such issues. This requires continuing courage and earnestness on your part to believe strongly in the power of karma and destiny to bring you the best.

Romance and friendship

Between the 2nd and 4th you must set an appropriate example in love. If you are a family person, others will learn from what they see. Particularly if you have children, your behaviour will be watched very closely and scrutinised in every manner. Your actions will speak much louder than words to those you love.

Remember that reputation is everything on the 9th. Don't go against the grain of your peers. You must act like others, even if you choose to think very differently. Stepping outside of the mould could make you a target for your enemies. It's your call; but if you do go your own way, you can expect some flak.

Someone will be unable to join you in a social event that you were looking forward to between the 14th and 16th, putting your attendance in jeopardy. Just go with the flow and try to find an alternative source of entertainment or amusement.

Between the 20th and 23rd you'll be able to speak eloquently and influence others somehow. You may not even be aware of your impact, but you'll certainly inspire and motivate them in an unusual way.

From the 25th to the 29th, interpret the words of your lover and friends correctly. Could I suggest you look more closely at their motives; at what they do rather than what they say?

On the 30th go out of your way to lend a helping hand or offer a lift to someone who is stuck. Playing the Good Samaritan will make you feel pretty good in yourself.

Work and money

You may need to make some additional journeys for work between the 1st and the 5th, and these will be quite tedious but profitable as well. Rather than merely enduring the trip and complaining about it, engage yourself with strangers who may even offer you new opportunities. Life tends to bring you great things in the strangest places in the most unusual ways, so remain receptive!

A change in policy or perhaps even a quick exit by an employer or staff member is likely from the 10th to the 15th. You may have to reassess your schedule due to these impromptu changes.

The powerful Sun shines its lucky vibes on your work after the 23rd and brings with it a peak of activity.

If you are an independent agent or run your own business, perhaps even from home, your company affairs should start to become profitable.

From the 28th to the 31st, important meetings mustn't be missed. Crucial information needs to be gained from these sources, otherwise you'll be 'left behind the eight ball'.

Destiny dates

Positive: 20, 22, 23

Negative: 5, 16, 17

Mixed: 1, 2, 3, 4, 9, 10, 11, 12, 13, 14, 15, 21, 25, 26, 27, 28, 29, 30, 31

NOVEMBER

Highlights of the month

This is an excellent time to commence a new project as the new Moon occurs in your zone of professionalism and self-development. Karma continues to bless you with opportunities and of course you must take them and not be shy in moving forward.

Between the 1st and the 7th you won't feel all that comfortable sitting around doing nothing and will want to pursue your goals actively without wasting too much time. You'll also be spurring on your friends in their own particular paths, or perhaps trying to illicit their help to gain an edge by using numbers as part of your strategy.

Finances should take a turn for the better, with Mars dynamically energising your profit sector. With the Sun trailing Jupiter in your finance sector, your independent business, if you have one, should start to see some better figures on the bottom line. For those of you who work for others, this is also a good time to increase your bank balance and look forward to some surplus cash.

Try to go easy on your friends, especially if you see them living life in a way that is riddled with discrepancies and lapses in judgement. You mustn't judge them too harshly. A kind word from you is more likely to give them the encouragement they need to help solve their personal problems. Personal affairs should be much less muddled after the 19th, when Venus goes direct.

Venus re-enters your zone of career after the 30th. This means that a postponement, or situation you thought may have been lost, may return and give you a 'second bite at the cherry', so to speak. This could also be favourable news for a sibling or someone close to you such as a relative or neighbour. There could be cause for celebration and a raising of the champagne glasses around this time.

Finally, it's important for you to put to bed any private concerns you have relating to health. An old injury, something that's bothered you for some time, may have been overlooked or dismissed as not that important by you. I don't want to alarm you, but even if, at this point, the malady is not all that troublesome, over time if left unchecked it could develop into something more serious. It's best to nip these issues in the bud when and as they arise, thereby short-circuiting any further complications.

Romance and friendship

Don't fight the status quo between the 3rd and the 6th. Relax! If what you are trying to achieve in your personal life isn't happening as quickly as you would like it to, why not then enjoy your own company and overcome a fear of being alone? You must love yourself first before you can accept that others love you.

Neptune, the planet of ideals, is in its march forward after the 7th. It's likely you'll feel physically alert and more able to pinpoint what to do to gain the upper hand in your relationship. This is a case of making your ideals a reality.

You'll visit a number of interesting places after the 10th. Your social life will be very engaging, bringing with it humour, joy and effervescent, lively interactions with others.

Between the 11th and 14th, 'fortune favours the brave'. Dare to confront your fears and mix with people who would otherwise seem out of your reach. You'll be attracted to some powerful or charismatic figure at this time. Lucky you!

Jupiter and Venus jointly move in direct motion and reflect lucky times in love. From the 19th to the 22nd is an important time to let down your hair and forget about convention, even if others frown upon you. It's all about you now. Fun, fun and more fun!

You'll feel compassionate with friends between the 23rd and the 27th, but need to be forceful in doling out your advice. Sometimes you have to be cruel to be kind; what's the point of spending inordinate amounts of time with people who aren't going to take to heart what you say?

Work and money

You'll be respected and honoured for your valuable contributions at work between the 5th and 8th. If you have some meaningful and intelligent ideas, make sure you copyright these assets before sharing them with anyone else. They are probably worth more than you think.

Your weapon of choice between the 9th and 12th should be words. Carefully constructed arguments are going to give you power over your competitors. You also have allies socially who will be prepared to give you a leg up in areas of work and finance.

A new pathway will be presented to you between the 14th and 17th, but you are ill-advised to act on a knee jerk response. You must think very carefully before you leap into a commitment.

Growing your assets may require you to consider real estate and other more traditional forms of investment between the 19th and 28th. You could be intrigued and will want to learn more.

Destiny dates

Positive: 1, 2, 3, 4, 5, 6, 7, 8, 9, 10, 11, 12, 13, 19, 20, 21, 22, 28, 30

Negative: none

Mixed: 14, 15, 16, 17, 23, 24, 25, 26, 27

DECEMBER

Highlights of the month

The whole idea of karma is to remind you that the past does eventually catch up with you. Depending on the nature of your deeds, your thoughts and your words, they will in time come to fruition and either bless you or curse you. This is your theme for the last month of 2010, because December commences with the combined influence of the Moon and Saturn in your zone of past karma.

One of the ideas I'd like to drive home to you in this closing phase of 2010 is that you can't do very much about the past: what's done is done. But if you do have an outstanding obligation, a moral responsibility, or something that has been left unsaid or unfinished, this is the time to deal with it.

Apologies—saying sorry—are not so much for the victim as for yourself, and it's important to let go of feelings of guilt or grief or any grudges that may be lurking within your heart. By removing these emotions from your mental and spiritual landscape, you'll find a much greater clarity and sense of purpose to your life.

I'm raising these issues particularly in connection with Mars moving into your quiet, spiritual and self-reflective zone on the 8th. It will remain here for a little while, giving you the opportunity to clean up your spiritual 'cupboards' and make amends; both with others, but more importantly, with yourself.

The lunar eclipse on the 21st is a powerful antidote to any of the problems you may have experienced and indicates that the future karma for Aquarians is marked for a special destiny. Love, children and creativity again take centre stage, and what a perfect time for it to do so, given that Christmas is just a few days away?

Put your full life force and vitality as well as your creativity into making Christmas a happy and joyous time for all of those concerned. Put aside your cynicism, even though I understand it's easy to believe that this time of the year is simply one of commercialism.

Romance and friendship

Venus occupies the upper part of your horoscope in December, so love and friendship will dominate most of your activities. Don't let your mood swings impact on your love life on the 1st. The period of the 3rd to the 5th is great for deepening the bonds of friendship.

If you've been unfortunate enough to be dealing with a stalled relationship, this love affair may be restarted suddenly between the 7th and 10th. Remember not to try too hard because others may judge you harshly for doing so.

Travel a highway to share your love with someone special after the 14th. Nature reserves or places with spectacular scenery will enhance your romantic feelings. Keep your private affairs close to your chest.

A friend will probe you to reveal an innermost secret. Don't give in!

A lunar eclipse on the 19th proves that you may have been blind in love. 'The truth will set you free', even if there is some temporary pain associated with the knowledge that is revealed. The truth is sometimes quite a difficult pill to swallow.

Bonding with loved ones is spotlighted between the 23rd and 29th. Active engagement in Christmas festivities, organising events and other social get-togethers will all be very pleasant.

You are loving and satisfied with your lot generally, especially by the 31st.

Work and money

'Vent your spleen' from the 3rd to the 6th. Holding in your opinions is not good for your health. If you know something inappropriate is happening, it's your duty to say something about it.

You'll perform great work alone this month,

especially between the 7th and 10th, and this could be because you don't necessarily want to share the glory. Someone could be trying to muscle in on your turf at work, trying to stake their claim on the rewards. Anticipation is the secret of securing greater success and coming out as number one. You may have to be a little selfish to keep the ball in your hands.

You are bright, intelligent and quick off the mark between the 14th and 18th. Write down your ideas or it is likely you'll forget them.

You need to tie up loose ends between the 21st and 24th. Remember, a clean office will ensure a worry free Christmas and a satisfactory conclusion to your professional affairs in 2010. It may sound odd but a spring cleaning at this late stage of the year will be great mental and emotional therapy for you. May the stars shine on you and bless you with health, wealth and happiness.

Destiny dates

Positive: 7, 9, 10, 14, 15, 16, 17, 18, 25, 26, 27, 28, 29, 31

Negative: 1, 19

Mixed: 3, 4, 5, 6, 8, 21, 22, 23, 24

AQUARIUS

2010: Astronumerology

Much may be done in those little shreds and patches of time which every day produces, and which most men throw away.

—Charles Caleb Colton

The power behind your name

By adding the numbers of your name you can see which planet is ruling you. Each of the letters of the alphabet is assigned a number, which is listed below. These numbers are ruled by the planets. This is according to the ancient Chaldean system of numerology and is very different to the Pythagorean system to which many refer.

Each number is assigned a planet:

AIQJY	**=**	**1**	**Sun**
BKR	**=**	**2**	**Moon**
CGLS	**=**	**3**	**Jupiter**
DMT	**=**	**4**	**Uranus**
EHNX	**=**	**5**	**Mercury**
UVW	**=**	**6**	**Venus**
OZ	**=**	**7**	**Neptune**
FP	**=**	**8**	**Saturn**
—	**=**	**9**	**Mars**

Notice that the number 9 is not aligned with a letter because it is considered special. Once the numbers have been added you will see that a single planet rules your name and personal affairs. Many famous actors, writers and musicians change their names to attract the energy of a luckier planet. You can experiment with the list and try new names or add the letters of your second name to see how that vibration suits you. It's a lot of fun!

Here is an example of how to find out the power of your name. If your name is John Smith, calculate the ruling planet by assigning each letter to a number in the table like this:

J O H N S M I T H
1 7 5 5 3 4 1 4 5

Now add the numbers like this:

1 + 7 + 5 + 5 + 3 + 4 + 1 + 4 + 5 = 35

Then add 3 + 5 = 8

The ruling number of John Smith's name is 8, which is ruled by Saturn. Now study the name-number table to reveal the power of your name. The numbers 3 and 5 will also play a secondary role in John's character and destiny, so in this case you would also study the effects of Jupiter and Mercury.

Name-number table

Your name number	Ruling planet	Your name characteristics
1	**Sun**	Magnetic individual. Great energy and life force. Physically dynamic and sociable. Attracts good friends and individuals in powerful positions. Good government connections. Intelligent, impressive, flashy and victorious. A loyal number for relationships.
2	**Moon**	Soft, emotional nature. Changeable moods but psychic, intuitive senses. Imaginative nature and empathetic expression of feelings. Loves family, mother and home life. Night owl who probably needs more sleep. Success with the public and/or women.
3	**Jupiter**	Outgoing, optimistic number with lucky overtones. Attracts opportunities without trying. Good sense of timing. Religious or spiritual aspirations.

Your name number	Ruling planet	Your name characteristics
		Can investigate the meaning of life. Loves to travel and explore the world and people.
4	**Uranus**	Explosive character with many unusual aspects. Likes the untried and novel. Forward thinking, with many extraordinary friends. Gets fed up easily so needs plenty of invigorating experiences. Pioneering, technological and imaginative. Wilful and stubborn when wants to be. Unexpected events in life may be positive or negative.
5	**Mercury**	Quick-thinking mind with great powers of speech. Extremely vigorous life; always on the go and lives on nervous energy. Youthful attitude and never grows old. Looks younger than actual age. Young friends and humorous disposition. Loves reading and writing.
6	**Venus**	Delightful personality. Graceful and attractive character who cherishes friends

Your name number	Ruling planet	Your name characteristics
		and social life. Musical or artistic interests. Good for money making as well as abundant love affairs. Career in the public eye is possible. Loves family but is often overly concerned by friends.
7	**Neptune**	Intuitive, spiritual and self-sacrificing nature. Easily misled by those who need help. Loves to dream of life's possibilities. Has curative powers. Dreams are revealing and prophetic. Loves the water and will have many journeys in life. Spiritual aspirations dominate worldly desires.
8	**Saturn**	Hard-working, focused individual with slow but certain success. Incredible concentration and self-sacrifice for a goal. Money orientated but generous when trust is gained. Professional but may be a hard taskmaster. Demands

		highest standards and needs to learn to enjoy life a little more.
9	**Mars**	Fantastic physical drive and ambition. Sports and outdoor activities are keys to wellbeing. Confrontational. Likes to work and play just as hard. Caring and protective of family, friends and territory. Individual tastes in life but is also self-absorbed. Needs to listen to others' advice to gain greater success.

Your 2010 planetary ruler

Astrology and numerology are very intimately connected. As already shown, each planet rules over a number between 1 and 9. Both your name *and* your birth date are ruled by planetary energies.

Add the numbers of your birth date and the year in question to find out which planet will control the coming year for you.

For example, if you were born on the 12th of November, add the numerals 1 and 2 (12, your day of birth) and 1 and 1 (11, your month of birth) to the year in question, in this case 2010 (the current year), like this:

1 + 2 + 1 + 1 + 2 + 0 + 1 + 0 = 8

The planet ruling your individual karma for 2010 will be Saturn because this planet rules the number 8.

You can even take your ruling name-number as shown earlier and add it to the year in question to throw more light on your coming personal affairs, like this:

John Smith = 8

Year coming = 2010

8 + 2 + 0 + 1 + 0 = 11

1 + 1 = 2

Therefore, 2 is the ruling number of the combined name and date vibrations. Study the Moon's number 2 influence for 2010.

Outlines of the year number ruled by each planet are given below. Enjoy!

1 is the year of the Sun

Overview

The Sun is the brightest object in the heavens and rules number 1 and the sign of Leo. Because of this the coming year will bring you great success and popularity.

You'll be full of life and radiant vibrations and are more than ready to tackle your new nine-year cycle, which begins now. Any new projects you commence are likely to be successful.

Your health and vitality will be very strong and your stamina at its peak. Even if you happen to have the odd problem with your health, your recuperative power will be strong.

You have tremendous magnetism this year so social popularity won't be a problem for you. I see many new friends and lovers coming into your life. Expect loads of invitations to parties and fun-filled outings. Just don't take your health for granted as you're likely to burn the candle at both ends.

With success coming your way, don't let it go to your head. You must maintain humility, which will make you even more popular in the coming year.

Love and pleasure

This is an important cycle for renewing your love and connections with your family, particularly if you have children. The Sun is connected with the sign of Leo and therefore brings an increase in musical and theatrical activities. Entertainment and other creative hobbies will be high on your agenda and bring you a great sense of satisfaction.

Work

You won't have to make too much of an effort to be successful this year because the brightness of the Sun will draw opportunities to you. Changes in work are likely and, if you have been concerned that opportunities are few and far between, 2010 will be different. You can expect some sort of promotion or an increase in income because your employers will take special note of your skills and service orientation.

Improving your luck

Leo is the ruler of number 1 and, therefore, if you're born under this star sign, 2010 will be particularly lucky. For others, July and August, the months of Leo, will bring good fortune. The 1st, 8th, 15th and 22nd hours of Sundays especially will give you a unique sort of luck in any sort of competition or activities generally. Keep your eye out for those born under Leo as they may be able to contribute something to your life and may even have a karmic connection to you. This is a particularly important year for your destiny.

Your lucky numbers in this coming cycle are 1, 10, 19 and 28.

2 is the year of the Moon

Overview

There's nothing more soothing than the cool light of the full Moon on a clear night. The Moon is emotional and receptive and controls your destiny in 2010. If you're able to use the positive energies of the Moon, it will be a great year in which you can realign and improve your relationships, particularly with family members.

Making a commitment to becoming a better person and bringing your emotions under control will also dominate your thinking. Try not to let your emotions get the better of you throughout the coming year because you may be drawn into the changeable nature of these lunar vibrations as well. If you fail to keep control of your emotional life you'll later regret some of your actions. You must blend careful thinking with feeling to arrive at the best results. Your luck throughout 2010 will certainly be determined by the state of your mind.

Because the Moon and the sign of Cancer rule the number 2 there is a certain amount of change to be expected this year. Keep your feelings steady and don't let your heart rule your head.

Love and pleasure

Your primary concern in 2010 will be your home and family life. You'll be finally keen to take on those renovations, or work on your garden. You may even think of buying a new home. You can at last carry out some of those plans and make your dreams come true. If you find yourself a little more temperamental than usual, do some extra meditation and spend time alone until you sort this out. You mustn't withhold your feelings from your partner as this will only create frustration.

Work

During 2010 your focus will be primarily on feelings and family; however, this doesn't mean you can't make great strides in your work as well. The Moon rules the general public and what you might find is that special opportunities and connections with the world at large present themselves to you. You could be working with large numbers of people.

If you're looking for a better work opportunity, try to focus your attention on women who can give you a hand. Use your intuition as it will be finely tuned this year. Work and career success depends upon your instincts.

Improving your luck

The sign of Cancer is your ruler this year and because the Moon rules Mondays, both this day of the week and the month of July are extremely lucky for you. The 1st, 8th, 15th and 22nd hours on Mondays will be very powerful. Pay special attention to the new and full Moon days throughout 2010.

The numbers 2, 11 and 29 are lucky for you.

3 is the year of Jupiter

Overview

The year 2010 will be a number 3 year for you and, because of this, Jupiter and Sagittarius will dominate your affairs. This is extremely lucky and shows you'll be motivated to broaden your horizons, gain more money and become extremely popular in your social circles. It looks like 2010 will be a fun-filled year with much excitement.

Jupiter and Sagittarius are generous to a fault and so, likewise, your open-handedness will mark the year. You'll be friendly and helpful to all of those around you.

Pisces is also under the rulership of the number 3 and this brings out your spiritual and compassionate nature. You'll become a much better person, reducing your negative karma by increasing your self-awareness and spiritual feelings. You will want to share your luck with those you love.

Love and pleasure

Travel and seeking new adventures will be part and parcel of your romantic life this year. Travelling to distant lands and meeting unusual people will open your heart to fresh possibilities of romance.

You'll try novel and audacious things and will find yourself in a different circle of friends. Compromise will be important in making your existing relationships work. Talk about your feelings. If you are currently in a relationship you'll feel an upswing in your affection for your partner. This is a perfect opportunity to deepen your love for each other and take your relationship to a new level.

If you're not yet attached to someone, there's good news for you. Great opportunities lie in store and a spiritual or karmic connection may be experienced in 2010.

Work

Great fortune can be expected through your working life in the next twelve months. Your friends and work colleagues will want to help you achieve your goals. Even your employers will be amenable to your requests for extra money or a better position within the organisation.

If you want to start a new job or possibly begin an independent line of business, this is a great year to do it. Jupiter looks set to give you plenty of opportunities, success and a superior reputation.

Improving your luck

As long as you can keep a balanced view of things and not overdo anything, your luck will increase dramatically throughout 2010. The important thing is to remain grounded and not be too airy-fairy about your objectives. Be realistic about your talents and capabilities and don't brag about your skills or achievements. This will only invite envy from others.

Moderate your social life as well and don't drink or eat too much as this will slow your reflexes and weaken your chances for success.

You have plenty of spiritual insights this year so you should use them to their maximum. In the 1st, 8th, 15th and 24th hours of Thursdays you should use your intuition to enhance your luck, and the numbers 3, 12, 21 and 30 are also lucky for you. March and December are your lucky months but generally the whole year should go pretty smoothly for you.

4 is the year of Uranus

Overview

The electric and exciting planet of the zodiac, Uranus, and its sign of Aquarius, rule your affairs throughout 2010. Dramatic events will surprise and at the same time unnerve you in your professional and personal life. So be prepared!

You'll be able to achieve many things this year and your dreams are likely to come true, but you mustn't be distracted or scattered with your energies. You'll be breaking through your own self-limitations and this will present challenges from your family and friends. You'll want to be independent and develop your spiritual powers and nothing will stop you.

Try to maintain discipline and an orderly lifestyle so you can make the most of these special energies this year. If unexpected things do happen, it's not a bad idea to have an alternative plan so you don't lose momentum.

Love and pleasure

You want something radical, something different in your relationships this year. It's quite likely that your love life will be feeling a little less than exciting so you'll take some important steps to change that. If your partner is as progressive as you'll be this year, then your relationship is likely to improve and fulfil both of you.

In your social life you will meet some very unusual people, whom you'll feel are especially connected to you spiritually. You may want to ditch everything for the excitement and passion of a completely new relationship, but tread carefully as this may not work out exactly as you expect it to.

Work

Technology, computing and the Internet will play a larger role in your professional life this coming year.

You'll have to move ahead with the times and learn new skills if you want to achieve success.

A hectic schedule is likely, so make sure your diary is with you at all times. Try to be more efficient and don't waste time.

New friends and alliances at work will help you achieve even greater success in the coming period. Becoming a team player will be even more important in gaining satisfaction from your professional endeavours.

Improving your luck

Moving too quickly and impulsively will cause you problems on all fronts, so be a little more patient and think your decisions through more carefully. Social, romantic and professional opportunities will come to you but take a little time to investigate the ramifications of your actions.

The 1st, 8th, 15th and 20th hours of any Saturday are lucky, but love and luck are likely to cross your path when you least expect it. The numbers 4, 13, 22 and 31 are also lucky for you this year.

5 is the year of Mercury

Overview

The supreme planet of communication, Mercury, is your ruling planet throughout 2010. The number 5, which is connected to Mercury, will confer upon you success through your intellectual abilities.

Any form of writing or speaking will be improved and this will be, to a large extent, underpinning your success. Your imagination will be stimulated by this planet, with many incredible new and exciting ideas coming to mind.

Mercury and the number 5 are considered somewhat indecisive. Be firm in your attitude and don't let too many ideas or opportunities distract and confuse you. By all means get as much information as you can to help you make the right decisions.

I see you involved with money proposals, job applications, even contracts that need to be signed, so remain as clear-headed as possible.

Your business skills and clear and concise communication will be at the heart of your life in 2010.

Love and pleasure

Mercury, which rules the signs of Gemini and Virgo, will make your love life a little difficult due to its changeable nature. On the one hand you'll feel passionate and loving to your partner, yet on the other you will feel like giving it all up for the excitement of a new affair. Maintain the middle ground.

Also, try not to be too critical with your friends and family members. The influence of Virgo makes you prone to expecting much more from others than they're capable of giving. Control your sharp tongue and don't hurt people's feelings. Encouraging others is the better path, leading to greater emotional satisfaction.

Work

Speed will dominate your professional life in 2010. You'll be flitting from one subject to another and taking on far more than you can handle. You'll need to make some serious changes in your routine to handle the avalanche of work that will come your way. You'll also be travelling with your work, but not necessarily overseas.

If you're in a job you enjoy then this year will give you additional successes. If not, it may be time to move on.

Improving your luck

Communication is the key to attaining your desires in the coming twelve months. Keep focused on one idea rather than scattering your energies in all directions and your success will be speedier.

By looking after your health, sleeping well and exercising regularly, you'll build up your resilience and mental strength.

The 1st, 8th, 15th and 20th hours of Wednesday are lucky so it's best to schedule your meetings and other important social engagements during these times. The lucky numbers for Mercury are 5, 14, 23 and 32.

6 is the year of Venus

Overview

Because you're ruled by 6 this year, love is in the air! Venus, Taurus and Libra are well known for their affinity with romance, love, and even marriage. If ever you were going to meet a soulmate and feel comfortable in love, 2010 must surely be your year.

Taurus has a strong connection to money and practical affairs as well, so finances will also improve if you are diligent about work and security issues.

The important thing to keep in mind this year is that sharing love and making that important soul connection should be kept high on your agenda. This will be an enjoyable period in your life.

Love and pleasure

Romance is the key thing for you this year and your current relationships will become more fulfilling if you happen to be attached. For singles, a 6 year heralds an important meeting that eventually leads to marriage.

You'll also be interested in fashion, gifts, jewellery and all sorts of socialising. It's at one of these social engagements that you could meet the love of your life. Remain available!

Venus is one of the planets that has a tendency to overdo things, so be moderate in your eating and drinking. Try generally to maintain a modest lifestyle.

Work

You'll have a clearer insight into finances and your future security during a number 6 year. Whereas previously you may have had additional expenses and extra distractions, your mind will now be more settled and capable of longer-term planning along these lines.

With the extra cash you might see this year, decorating your home or office will give you a special sort of satisfaction.

Social affairs and professional activities will be strongly linked. Any sort of work-related functions may offer you romantic opportunities as well. On the other hand, be careful not to mix up your workplace relationships with romantic ideals. This could complicate some of your professional activities.

Improving your luck

You'll want more money and a life of leisure and ease in 2010. Keep working on your strengths and eliminate your negative personality traits to create greater luck and harmony in your life.

Moderate all your actions and don't focus exclusively on money and material objects. Feed your spiritual needs as well. By balancing your inner and outer sides you'll see that your romantic and professional lives will be enhanced more easily.

The 1st, 8th, 15th and 20th hours on Fridays will be very lucky for you and new opportunities will arise for you at those times. You can use the numbers 6, 15, 24 and 33 to increase luck in your general affairs.

7 is the year of Neptune

Overview

The last and most evolved sign of the zodiac is

Pisces, which is ruled by Neptune. The number 7 is deeply connected with this zodiac sign and governs you in 2010. Your ideals seem to be clearer and more spiritually orientated than ever before. Your desire to evolve and understand your inner self will be a double-edged sword. It depends on how organised you are as to how well you can use these spiritual and abstract concepts in your practical life.

Your past hurts and deep emotional issues will be dealt with and removed for good, if you are serious about becoming a better human being.

Spend a little more time caring for yourself rather than others, as it's likely some of your friends will drain you of energy with their own personal problems. Of course, you mustn't turn a blind eye to the needs of others, but don't ignore your own personal requirements in the process.

Love and pleasure

Meeting people with similar life views and spiritual aspirations will rekindle your faith in relationships. If you do choose to develop a new romance, make sure there is a clear understanding of the responsibilities of one to the other. Don't get swept off your feet by people who have ulterior motives.

Keep your relationships realistic and see that the most idealistic partnerships must eventually come down to Earth. Deal with the practicalities of life.

Work

This is a year of hard work, but one in which you'll

come to understand the deeper significance of your professional ideals. You may discover a whole new aspect to your career, which involves a more compassionate and self-sacrificing side to your personality.

You'll also find that your way of working will change and you'll be more focused and able to get into the spirit of whatever you do. Finding meaningful work is very likely and therefore this could be a year when money, security, creativity and spirituality overlap to bring you a great sense of personal satisfaction.

Tapping into your greater self through meditation and self-study will bring you great benefits throughout 2010.

Improving your luck

Using self-sacrifice along with discrimination will be an unusual method of improving your luck. The laws of karma state that what you give, you receive in greater measure. This is one of the principal themes for you in 2010.

The 1st, 8th, 15th and 20th hours of Tuesdays are your lucky times. The numbers 7, 16, 25 and 34 should be used to increase your lucky energies.

8 is the year of Saturn

Overview

The earthy and practical sign of Capricorn and its ruler Saturn are intimately linked to the number

8, which rules you in 2010. Your discipline and far-sightedness will help you achieve great things in the coming year. With cautious discernment, slowly but surely you will reach your goals.

It may be that due to the influence of the solitary Saturn, your best work and achievement will be behind closed doors away from the limelight. You mustn't fear this as you'll discover many new things about yourself. You'll learn just how strong you really are.

Love and pleasure

Work will overshadow your personal affairs in 2010, but you mustn't let this erode the personal relationships you have. Becoming a workaholic brings great material successes but will also cause you to become too insular and aloof. Your family members won't take too kindly to you working 100-hour weeks.

Responsibility is one of the key words for this number and you will therefore find yourself in a position of authority that leaves very little time for fun. Try to make the time to enjoy the company of friends and family and by all means schedule time off on the weekends as it will give you the peace of mind you're looking for.

Because of your responsible attitude it will be very hard for you not to assume a greater role in your workplace and this indicates longer working hours with the likelihood of a promotion with equally good remuneration.

Work

Money is high on your agenda in 2010. Number 8 is a good money number according to the Chinese and this year is at last likely to bring you the fruits of your hard labour. You are cautious and resourceful in all your dealings and will not waste your hard-earned savings. You will also be very conscious of using your time wisely.

You will be given more responsibilities and you're likely to take them on, if only to prove to yourself that you can handle whatever life dishes up.

Expect a promotion in which you'll play a leading role in your work. Your diligence and hard work will pay off, literally, in a bigger salary and more respect from others.

Improving your luck

Caution is one of the key characteristics of the number 8 and is linked to Capricorn. But being overly cautious could cause you to miss valuable opportunities. If an offer is put to you, try to think outside the square and balance it with your naturally cautious nature.

Be gentle and kind to yourself. By loving yourself, others will naturally love you, too. The 1st, 8th, 15th and 20th hours of Saturdays are exceptionally lucky for you, as are the numbers 1, 8, 17, 26 and 35.

9 is the year of Mars

Overview

You are now entering the final year of a nine-year cycle dominated by the planet Mars and the sign of Aries. You'll be completing many things and are determined to be successful after several years of intense work.

Some of your relationships may now have reached their use-by date and even personal affairs may need to be released. Don't let arguments and disagreements get in the road of friendly resolution in these areas of your life.

Mars is a challenging planet, and this year, although you will be very active and productive, you may find others trying to obstruct the achievement of your goals. As a result you may react strongly to them, thereby creating disharmony in your workplace. Don't be so impulsive or reckless, and generally slow things down. The slower, steadier approach has greater merit this year.

Love and pleasure

If you become too bossy and pushy with friends this year you will just end up pushing them out of your life. It's a year to end certain friendships but by the same token it could be the perfect time to remove conflicts and thereby bolster your love affairs in 2010.

If you're feeling a little irritable and angry with those you love, try getting rid of these negative feelings through some intense, rigorous sports and physical activity. This will definitely relieve tension and improve your personal life.

Work

Because you're healthy and able to work at a more intense pace you'll achieve an incredible amount in the coming year. Overwork could become a problem if you're not careful.

Because the number 9 and Mars are infused with leadership energy, you'll be asked to take the reins of the job and steer your company or group in a certain direction. This will bring with it added responsibility but also a greater sense of purpose for you.

Improving your luck

Because of the hot and restless energy of the number 9, it is important to create more mental peace in your life this year. Lower the temperature, so to speak, and decompress your relationships rather than becoming aggravated. Try to talk with your work partners and loved ones rather than telling them what to do. This will generally pick up your health and your relationships.

The 1st, 8th, 15th and 20th hours of Tuesdays are the luckiest for you this year and, if you're involved in any disputes or need to attend to health issues, these times are also very good to get the best results. Your lucky numbers are 9, 18, 27 and 36.

AQUARIUS

2010:
Your Daily Planner

Happiness is often the result of being too busy to be miserable.

—Anonymous

According to astrology, the success of any venture or activity is dependent upon the planetary positions at the time you commence that activity. Electional astrology helps you select the most appropriate times for many of your day-to-day endeavours. These dates are applicable to each and every zodiac sign and can be used freely by one and all, even if your star sign doesn't fall under the one mentioned in this book. Please note that the daily planner is a universal system applicable equally to all *twelve* star signs. Anyone and everyone can use this planner irrespective of their birth sign.

Ancient astrologers understood the planetary patterns and how they impacted on each of us. This allowed them to suggest the best possible times to start various important activities. For example, many farmers still use this approach today: they understand the phases of the Moon, and attest to the fact that planting seeds on certain lunar days produces a far better crop than does planting on other days.

In the following section, many facets of daily life are considered. Using the lunar cycle and the combined strength of other planets allows us to work out the best times to do them. This is your personal almanac, which can be used in conjunction with any star sign to help optimise the results.

First, select the activity you are interested in, and then quickly scan the year for the best months to start it. When you have selected the month, you can finetune your timing by finding the best specific dates. You can then be sure that the planetary energies will be in sync with you, offering you the best possible outcome.

Coupled with what you know about your monthly and weekly trends, the daily planner is an effective tool to help you capitalise on opportunities that come your way this year.

Good luck, and may the planets bless you with great success, fortune and happiness in 2010!

Getting started in 2010

How many times have you made a new year's resolution to begin a diet or be a better person in your relationships? And, how many times has it not worked out? Well, part of the reason may be that you started out at the wrong time, because how successful you are is strongly influenced by the position of the Moon and the planets when you begin a particular activity. You will be more successful with the following endeavours if you start them on the days indicated.

Relationships

We all feel more empowered on some days than on others. This is because the planets have some power over us—their movement and their relationships to each other determine the ebb and flow of our energies. And, our levels of self-confidence and sense of romantic magnetism play an important part in the way we behave in relationships.

Your daily planner tells you the ideal dates for meeting new friends, initiating a love affair, spending time with family and loved ones—it even tells you the most appropriate times for sexual encounters.

You'll be surprised at how much more impact you will make in your relationships when you tune yourself in to the planetary energies on these special dates.

Falling in love/restoring love

During these times you could expect favourable energies to meet your soulmate or, if you've had difficulty in a relationship, to approach the one you love to rekindle both your and their emotional responses:

January	18, 20, 23, 24
February	15, 16, 20, 24
March	29
April	16
May	14, 17, 18, 19, 20, 23
June	14, 15, 16, 20, 21
July	12
August	10, 13, 14
September	9, 21, 22
October	8, 18, 19, 20
November	14, 15, 16, 19, 20, 21
December	13, 17, 18

Special times with friends and family

Socialising, partying and having a good time with those whose company you enjoy is highly favourable under the following dates. They are excellent to spend time with family and loved ones in a domestic environment:

January	6, 26, 27
February	12, 13, 14, 15, 16, 20, 24
March	11, 21, 22, 29, 30, 31
April	8
May	15, 16, 17, 18, 19, 20, 23, 24
June	1, 2, 3, 11, 12, 14, 15, 16, 20, 21, 29, 30
July	8, 9, 12, 17, 18, 26, 27
August	5, 6, 9, 10, 13, 14, 22, 23, 24
September	1, 2, 5, 9, 10, 18, 19, 20, 30
October	3, 19, 20, 25, 26, 30, 31
November	3, 4, 14, 15, 16, 22, 26, 27
December	2, 9, 10, 11, 19, 20, 24, 25

Healing or resuming relationships

If you're trying to get back together with the one you love or need a heart-to-heart or deep-and-meaningful discussion with someone, you can try the following dates to do so:

January	12, 13, 14, 15, 21, 22, 23, 24, 25
February	6
March	6, 31
April	2, 7, 8, 12, 16, 19, 23, 24, 25, 26

May	10, 11, 12, 13, 14, 15, 16, 17, 18, 19, 20, 21,22, 23, 24, 25, 26, 27, 28, 30
June	3, 8, 9, 10, 11, 12, 13, 14, 15, 16, 17, 21, 22, 23, 25, 26, 27, 28, 29, 30
July	1, 2, 3, 4, 5, 10, 11, 12, 13, 15, 16, 17, 18, 19, 20, 21, 22, 23, 28, 29, 30
August	1, 2, 3, 4, 5, 6, 9, 10, 13, 14, 15, 16, 20, 23, 25, 26, 27
September	2, 5, 9, 10, 13, 17, 18, 19, 20
October	1, 2, 3, 6, 12, 13, 14, 15, 20, 22, 23, 24, 25, 26, 27, 28, 29, 30, 31
November	3, 4, 5, 6, 7, 8, 9, 21, 27, 28, 29, 30
December	2, 3, 4, 6, 12, 13, 14, 17, 18, 19, 20, 21, 23, 24, 25

Sexual encounters

Physical and sexual energies are well favoured on the following dates. The energies of the planets enhance your moments of intimacy during these times:

January	1, 6, 7, 21, 22
February	6, 12, 13, 14, 20, 24
March	14, 15, 17, 18, 19, 30, 31
April	23, 24, 25, 26
May	9, 12, 14, 17, 18, 19, 20
June	3, 8, 9, 10, 11, 14, 15, 16, 20, 21, 29, 30
July	8, 9, 10, 11, 12
August	6, 10, 13, 14, 22, 23, 24

September	3, 4, 5, 6, 9, 10, 18, 19, 20, 21, 22, 30
October	1, 2, 3, 7, 8, 18, 19, 20, 23, 24, 28, 29, 30, 31
November	3, 4, 14, 15, 16, 19, 24, 25, 26, 27
December	2, 10, 11, 12, 13, 15, 16, 17, 19, 20, 22, 23, 24, 25

Health and wellbeing

Your aura and life force are susceptible to the movements of the planets—in particular, they respond to the phases of the Moon.

The following dates are the most appropriate times to begin a diet, have cosmetic surgery, or seek medical advice. They also indicate the best times to help others.

Feeling of wellbeing

Your physical as well as your mental alertness should be strong on these following dates. You can plan your activities and expect a good response from others:

January	2, 3, 4, 5, 6, 7, 11, 12, 13, 14, 16, 17, 18, 21, 22, 23, 24, 30, 31
February	1, 2, 7, 8, 15, 16, 17, 18, 19, 20, 21, 22, 23, 24, 25, 26, 27, 28
March	16, 17, 18, 19, 20, 22, 23, 24, 25, 26, 27, 28, 29
April	7, 13, 14, 16, 28
May	2, 11, 14, 25, 26
June	8, 22, 23, 26, 27, 28, 29, 30

July	4, 5, 8, 9, 12, 13, 14, 15, 16, 19, 20, 23, 24, 25
August	5, 6, 9, 10, 11, 12, 13, 15, 16, 20, 21
September	9, 10, 11, 12, 13, 16, 17, 21, 22, 24, 25, 28, 29, 30
October	3, 4, 5, 6, 7, 8, 9, 10, 13, 14, 15, 22
November	4, 5, 6, 10, 11, 19, 20, 21
December	7, 8, 17, 18, 28, 29

Healing and medicine

These times are good for approaching others who have expertise when you need some deeper understanding. They are also favourable for any sort of healing or medication and making appointments with doctors or psychologists. Planning surgery around these dates should bring good results.

Often giving up our time and energy to assist others doesn't necessarily result in the expected outcome. However, by lending a helping hand to a friend on the following dates, the results should be favourable:

January	1, 2, 3, 4, 6, 7, 8, 9, 11, 12, 13, 14, 15, 16, 17, 18, 19, 20, 21, 22, 23, 24, 26, 27, 28, 29, 30, 31
February	1, 5, 6, 9, 11, 12, 13, 14, 15, 16, 19
March	1, 2, 3, 4, 5, 8, 9, 10, 11, 12, 18, 19, 24, 25, 29
April	1, 3, 4, 5, 22, 26
May	4, 5

June	1, 2, 3, 9, 10, 17, 18, 22, 23, 24, 25, 29, 30
July	6, 7, 15, 16, 17, 18, 19, 21, 22, 23, 24, 25, 26
August	2, 3, 4, 11, 12, 17, 18, 19, 20, 21, 30, 31
September	6, 7, 8, 10, 11, 12, 13, 14, 15, 16, 17, 18, 26, 27, 28, 29
October	5, 7, 8, 9, 10, 11, 12, 13, 14, 15, 16, 17, 18, 19, 20, 21, 22, 23, 24, 25, 26, 28, 29, 30, 31
November	1, 2, 3, 5, 7, 8, 10, 11, 14, 15, 17, 18, 19, 22, 23
December	4, 5, 7, 8, 9, 10, 12, 13, 14, 16, 23, 24, 25, 26, 28, 29, 30, 31

Money

Money is an important part of life, and involves many decisions—decisions about borrowing, investing, spending. The ideal times for transactions are very much influenced by the planets, and whether your investment or nest egg grows or doesn't grow can often be linked to timing. Making your decisions on the following dates could give you a whole new perspective on your financial future.

Managing wealth and money

To build your nest egg it's a good time to open your bank account or invest money on the following dates:

January	1, 6, 7, 13, 14, 15, 18, 21, 22, 28, 29
February	3, 4, 9, 10, 11, 12, 13, 14, 15, 17, 18, 24, 25

March	2, 3, 9, 10, 16, 17, 18, 23, 24, 29, 30, 31
April	5, 6, 7, 13, 14, 19, 20, 21, 26, 27,
May	2, 3, 4, 10, 11, 17, 18, 23, 24, 30, 31
June	6, 7, 8, 13, 14, 19, 20, 21, 26, 27, 28
July	4, 5, 10, 11, 12, 17, 18, 23, 24, 25, 31
August	1, 7, 8, 13, 14, 20, 21, 27, 28, 29
September	3, 4, 9, 10, 16, 17, 23, 24, 25
October	1, 2, 7, 8, 13, 14, 15, 21, 22, 28, 29
November	3, 4, 10, 11, 17, 18, 24, 25
December	1, 2, 7, 8, 14, 15, 16, 21, 22, 23, 24, 29

Spending

It's always fun to spend but the following dates are more in tune with this activity and are likely to give you better results:

January	3, 4, 5, 6, 7, 8, 9, 10, 11, 12, 13, 14
February	3, 4, 5, 10, 19
March	8, 10, 11, 13, 14, 19
April	7, 8, 11, 12, 22
May	6, 7, 8, 9, 10, 11, 12, 13, 17, 18, 19, 20, 21, 22, 23, 24, 25, 26, 27, 28
June	1, 11, 12, 14, 16, 17, 19, 23, 25, 26, 27, 28, 29, 30
July	6, 7, 8, 23, 24, 25, 26, 27, 28, 29, 31
August	1, 2, 3, 4, 5, 15, 16, 17, 18, 19, 30, 31
September	1, 2, 3, 4, 17, 18, 19, 20, 21, 22, 23, 27, 28, 29, 30

October	4, 7, 12, 13, 14, 15, 16, 17, 18, 19, 27, 28
November	2, 3, 4, 25, 26, 27, 28
December	11, 22, 23

Selling

If you're thinking of selling something, whether it is small or large, consider the following dates as ideal times to do so:

January	18
February	12, 13, 14, 15
March	5, 6, 9, 14, 15, 16, 17, 18, 19, 21
April	1, 3, 4, 5, 22, 26
May	7, 12, 21, 29
June	3, 8, 9, 10, 11, 12, 13, 17, 24, 25, 26, 27, 28, 30
July	1, 2, 7, 9, 10, 11, 25, 27, 28, 29, 30, 31
August	1, 2, 3, 4, 5, 6, 7, 8, 9, 10, 13, 20, 23, 28
September	2, 9, 10, 11, 12, 13, 14, 15, 16, 17, 18, 19, 20, 21, 22, 23, 24, 26, 30
October	1, 2, 3, 4, 6, 7, 10, 11, 17, 18, 19, 20, 21, 22, 23, 24, 25, 27, 29
November	3, 4, 5, 6, 7, 11, 14, 15, 16, 17, 18, 19, 21, 23, 24, 25, 26, 27, 28, 29, 30
December	1, 2, 3, 4, 5, 6, 7, 8, 9, 10, 11, 12, 13, 14, 15, 16, 17, 18, 19, 20, 21, 22

Borrowing

Few of us like to borrow money, but if you must, taking out a loan on the following dates will be positive:

January	12, 30
February	7, 12, 13
March	6, 7, 8, 11
April	3, 4, 8
May	9, 28, 29
June	1, 2, 3, 4, 5, 29, 30
July	1, 2, 3, 26, 27, 28, 29, 30
August	9, 25, 26
September	5, 6
October	3, 30
November	26, 27
December	3, 4, 21, 22, 23, 30, 31

Work and education

Your career is important, and continual improvement of your skills is therefore also crucial professionally, mentally and socially. The dates below will help you find out the most appropriate times to improve your professional talents and commence new work or education associated with your work.

You may need to decide when to start learning a new skill, when to ask for a promotion, and even when to make an important career change. Here are the days when your mental and educational power is strong.

Learning new skills

Educational pursuits are lucky and bring good results on the following dates:

January	15, 16, 17, 18, 19, 20, 21, 22, 25, 26, 27
February	14, 15, 16, 17, 18, 19, 22, 23, 28
March	16, 17, 18, 21, 22, 27, 28
April	17, 18, 24, 25
May	15, 16, 21, 22
June	12, 17, 18, 24, 25
July	15, 16, 21, 22, 23, 24, 25
August	11, 12, 17, 18, 19
September	8, 13, 15, 20, 21, 22
October	11, 12
November	7, 8, 9
December	6, 19, 20

Changing career path or profession

If you're feeling stuck and need to move into a new professional activity, changing jobs could be done at these times:

January	6, 7, 15, 16, 17, 23, 24
February	12, 13, 14, 19, 20, 21
March	19, 20, 27, 28
April	15, 16, 24, 25
May	14, 21, 22
June	17, 18, 19, 20, 21
July	8, 9, 15, 16, 23, 24, 25

August	5, 6, 11, 12, 20, 21, 22, 23
September	1, 2, 8, 13, 14, 15, 17
October	8, 13, 14, 15, 16, 17
November	3, 4, 10, 11, 19, 20, 21
December	1, 2, 3, 7, 8, 17, 18, 28, 29

Promotion, professional focus and hard work

To increase your mental focus and achieve good results from the work you do; promotions are also likely on these dates:

January	4, 5, 6, 11, 12, 13, 14, 15, 16, 17, 18, 19, 21
February	6
March	16, 17, 18, 19, 20, 21, 23, 24, 25, 26, 27, 28, 29
April	8, 28, 29
May	12, 21
June	25, 26, 27, 28
July	4, 5, 8, 9, 12, 13, 14, 15, 16, 17, 18, 19, 20, 21, 22, 23, 24, 25, 26, 27
August	5, 6, 10, 11, 12, 13, 14, 15, 16, 17, 18, 19, 20, 21, 22, 23, 24
September	13, 14, 15
October	10, 11, 12, 13, 14, 15, 17, 18, 19, 20, 22, 23, 24, 30, 31
November	2, 4, 5, 6, 7, 8, 9, 23, 24, 25, 26, 27, 28, 29, 30
December	2, 3, 4, 11, 12, 13, 14, 15, 16, 18, 19, 20, 21, 23, 24, 25

Travel

Setting out on a holiday or adventurous journey is exciting. Here are the most favourable times for doing this. Travel on the following dates is likely to give you a sense of fulfilment:

January	15
February	15, 16, 18, 19, 20, 21
March	16, 17, 18, 21, 22, 23
April	19, 24, 25, 26, 27
May	16, 17, 18, 21, 22
June	17, 18, 19, 20, 21, 24, 25
July	21, 22, 23, 24, 25
August	19
September	9, 21, 22
October	18, 19, 20, 21, 22
November	7, 16, 17, 18
December	6, 14, 16, 19, 20

Beauty and grooming

Believe it or not, cutting your hair or nails has a powerful effect on your body's electromagnetic energy. If you cut your hair or nails at the wrong time of the month, you can reduce your level of vitality significantly. Use these dates to ensure you optimise your energy levels by staying in tune with the stars.

Hair and nails

January	1, 2, 3, 4, 5, 6, 7, 8, 11, 12, 13, 14, 15, 18, 19, 20, 21, 22, 25, 26, 27
February	3, 4, 5, 7, 8, 15, 16, 17, 18, 19, 22, 23, 24, 25
March	2, 3, 4, 6, 7, 8, 14, 15, 21, 22
April	1, 2, 3, 4, 5, 10, 11, 12, 17, 18, 19, 20, 21, 22, 23, 28, 29, 30
May	1, 2, 3, 4, 5, 7, 8, 9, 10, 11, 12, 13, 15, 16, 17, 18, 25, 26 27, 28, 29, 30
June	4, 5, 11, 12, 14, 15, 16, 24, 25
July	1, 2, 3, 8, 9, 12, 13, 14, 21, 22, 28, 29, 30
August	1, 2, 5, 6, 17, 18, 19, 25, 26
September	1, 2, 6, 7, 14, 15, 21, 22, 23, 24, 28, 29, 30
October	3, 4, 11, 12, 18, 19, 20, 25, 26, 27, 28, 29, 30
November	7, 8, 9, 14, 15, 16, 22, 23, 24, 25, 26, 27
December	5, 6, 12, 13, 19, 20, 21, 22, 23, 24, 25

Therapies, massage and self-pampering

January	6, 7, 13, 14, 15, 18, 19, 20, 21
February	2, 3, 9, 11, 14
March	1, 9, 14, 16, 17, 20, 23, 29
April	4, 5, 6, 10, 11, 12, 13, 17, 25, 26
May	2, 3, 7, 8, 9, 10, 11, 14, 15, 16, 17, 22, 23, 24, 31
June	3, 5, 12, 18, 19, 26, 27
July	4, 7, 8, 9, 10, 16, 23, 28, 29, 30, 31
August	3, 4, 5, 6, 7, 13, 20, 21, 24, 25, 26, 27, 28, 31
September	2, 17, 21, 28, 29

October	13, 14, 15, 18, 19, 21, 25, 26, 27, 28
November	2, 3, 9, 11, 14, 15, 16, 17, 21, 24, 29
December	7, 12, 13, 14, 15, 18, 19, 20, 22, 26, 27, 28, 29